ANGLO-SAXON

WEAPONS AND WARFARE

T0323026

ANGLO-SAXON
WEAPONS AND WARFARE

Richard Underwood

The History Press

First published 1999
First paperback edition 2001
Reprinted 2006, 2024

The History Press
97 St George's Place,
Cheltenham, Gloucestershire GL50 3QB
www.thehistorypress.co.uk

© Richard Underwood, 1999, 2001

The right of Richard Underwood to be identified as the Author
of this work has been asserted by him in accordance with the
Copyrights, Designs and Patents Act 1988.

All rights reserved. No part of this book may be reprinted
or reproduced or utilised in any form or by any electronic,
mechanical or other means, now known or hereafter invented,
including photocopying and recording, or in any information
storage or retrieval system, without the permission in writing
from the Publishers.

British Library Cataloguing in Publication Data.
A catalogue record for this book is available from the British Library.

ISBN 978 0 7524 1910 7

Typesetting and origination by Tempus Publishing.
Printed by TJ Books Limited, Padstow, Cornwall

Contents

The illustrations

Text figures

Colour Plates

Preface and acknowledgements

This book is primarily aimed at the re-enactor, wargamer, military historian or general reader. It aims to bring together information from a wide range of sources about the weapons and equipment used by Anglo-Saxon warriors during the centuries from the end of Roman Britain to the arrival of the Vikings (AD 450-800). The descriptions of the weapons include information on how they were used in battle and the core chapters on equipment are supplemented by chapters describing how warfare was organised and conducted.

My interest in Anglo-Saxon history began at university when I joined a re-enactment group known as 'The Arthurian Society', later renamed 'The English Settlement Society'. At the time I did not anticipate how this interest would grow, for the great fun of re-enactment is that, to be done properly, it inspires research into almost every aspect of a period of history, not only weapons and warfare but also cooking and cleaning (we once even experimented with re-enactment soap made from lard and wood ash, but only once). Since then, with a variety of groups, I have made, used and had used against me all of the equipment described in this book.

It is trite, but also true, to say that this book would not have been possible without the support of my partner Karen Dixon. She both proposed the under-taking and supported me throughout, as well as drawing the majority of the figures.

I would also like to thank Philip Clark for his help and advice, particularly the loan of the greater part of his library, Paul Mullis, who among other things provided most of the information on archery, Ian Stephenson and Ian Pain.

I am also indebted to Samantha Middleton of the Bowes Museum for all her help and advice including reviewing the text, to Richard Knox of Leicestershire Museums Service for the use of his illustrations, and to Keith Matthews of The York Castle Museum and Ian Meadows of Northamptonshire Archaeology for their assistance.

Photographs have been provided by the following organisations: Vojvodjanski Museum, Novi Sad; Archäologisches Landesmuseum, Schleswig; The National Museum, Copenhagan; Northamptonshire Archaeology; Sheffield City Museum; The York Castle Museum; The British Library; The British Museum; The Museum of London.

1 Introduction

Sources

Any historical study relies on two main sources of information: literary records and archaeology. In studying the weapons of the Anglo-Saxons we are extremely fortunate that they often chose to bury their dead with the weapons and armour that demonstrated their status as warriors (**1**). Few other areas of Anglo-Saxon study are as well supported by the archaeological record. Sufficient evidence exists not only to observe the development of the weapons over time, but even at times to chart the regional differences that existed.

However, when studying collections of artefacts recovered from graves, great care is essential. It is easy to fall into the trap of assuming that the grave goods with which the dead were buried represent a cross-section of their possessions in life. This is unlikely to be the case; the funerary rite is necessarily selective. The majority of weapon burials make little sense if they are viewed as a set. Graves are found with a shield but no weapons, or two shields. Clearly the pagan Anglo-Saxons chose, and chose carefully, the goods with which they furnished their graves. Unfortunately, we can only guess at their reasons.

To further complicate matters the frequency with which finds are made does not reflect the frequency with which they were deposited. Wood and leather only survive in waterlogged conditions and are rarely found except for small fragments adhering to metal objects and preserved by their corrosion products. In contrast, with the exception of small ferrous objects, metal tends to survive well in dry English soil.

When studying warfare, that is how and why the weapons were used, we must rely much more on literary records, which, unfortunately, give a far more fragmented picture. Direct literary evidence, written by the Anglo-Saxons about themselves, only began to be produced following their conversion to Christianity in the seventh century. There are three main types of writing: Christian writings, including histories and biographies of Anglo-Saxon saints, heroic poetry, and legal documents such as laws and wills.

Not surprisingly the bulk of Christian writings tell us little or nothing of Anglo-Saxon warfare being primarily concerned with spiritual matters. Of those that do the most important is the *Ecclesiastical History of the English People*, written by the Venerable

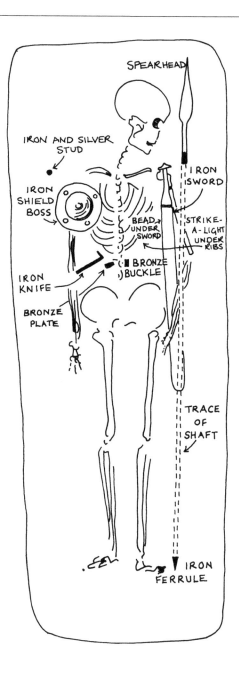

1   *Plan of the grave of a warrior from Petersfinger, Wiltshire. The pagan Anglo-Saxons often buried their dead with their personal posessions including their weapons. This practice ceased following their conversion to Christianity in the seventh century. As a consequence a great deal is known about the weapons and equipment of the fifth and sixth centuries whilst relatively little is known about the later period.*

(Drawn by K.R. Dixon after Leeds and Shortt)

Bede in AD 731. While largely devoted to the history of the Church, Bede also makes passing references to the major battles of his day, although as a cleric he is not overly interested in the detailed events of the battlefield. The other main source is the *Anglo-Saxon Chronicle*, compiled in the ninth century but drawing on earlier sources. Unfortunately, for the early period it rarely provides any detail beyond the participants and location of battles. Added to this the early accounts cannot be entirely trusted as they are influenced by a desire to explain, and to an extent vindicate, the origins of the later kingdoms, particularly Wessex. In addition to Anglo-Saxon works we also have those written by their British contemporaries, particularly Gildas and Nennius. All these works tend to have survived by frequent transcription of the manuscript, with editorial notes or glosses incorporated at each stage, making it difficult to separate the original work from later additions.

The most inspiring literary works of the Anglo-Saxons, their heroic poetry, was not designed to be written down, rather to perpetuate an oral record of events in a pre-literate society (**2**). It accomplished this by the careful interweaving of words, using meter and alliteration, attempting to bind them together into a single immutable whole. This was extremely effective, poems first written down in the eighth or ninth centuries may well have been composed in the sixth or even fifth century, but it was not without its drawbacks; it required the use of traditional formulae to provide links between phrases and the extensive use of synonyms and allusion, all of which makes separating the history from the art form extremely difficult.

Legal documents, law codes, wills and charters, provide our only unbiased evidence, albeit that the majority date from the late Saxon period. While often difficult to interpret, they provide direct evidence of the social organisation of military forces, although, by their nature, they do not tell us anything about the way in which war was conducted.

To supplement the direct literary evidence we are forced to draw on accounts of other Germanic societies, either from Roman or post-Roman sources, describing contemporary continental tribes such as the Franks or the Goths, or later Viking sources. Viking sources in particular frequently include detailed descriptions of warfare from individual combats to large battles. It should be recognised, however, that although most of the sagas deal with events between the ninth and eleventh centuries when the weapons and nature of war had probably changed little, they were in fact written down in the thirteenth and fourteenth centuries, and hence the descriptions may be anachronistic.

There is, therefore, a dilemma at the core of Anglo-Saxon studies. The early pagan Anglo-Saxons left ample physical evidence of their lives as a result of their practice of burying their dead with grave goods, yet they left no written record; once converted to Christianity and given the opportunity to record their lives with the written word they disdained the pagan practices of their forefathers, burying their dead without material possessions. As a consequence, we are repeatedly driven to interpret artefacts from the pagan period on the basis of much later written records, while the written history cannot generally be in any way verified by the evidence of archaeology.

2 *A page from the Beowulf manuscript (lines 1054-1075):*

(Photograph courtesy of The British Library)

golde forgyldan,   þone ðe Grendel ær
mane acwealde,   swa he hyra ma wolde,
nefne him witig god   wyde forstode
ond ðæs mannes mod.   Metod eallum weold
gumena cynnes,   swa he nu git deð.
Forþan bið andgit   æghwær selest,
ferhðes foreþanc.   Fela sceal gebidan
leofes ond laþes   se þe longe her
on ðyssum windagum   worolde bruceð
þær wæs sang ond sweg   samod ætgædere
fore Healfdenes   hildewisan,
gomenwudu greted,   gid oft wrecen
ðonne healgamen   Hroþgares scop
æfter medobence   mænan scolde
Finnes eaferum   ða hie se fær begeat,
hæleð Healfdena,   Hnæf Scyldinga,
in Freswæle   feallan scolde
Ne huru Hildeburh   herian þorfte
Eotena treowe;   unsynnum wearð
beloren leofum   æt þam lindplegan,
bearnum ond broðrum;   hie on gebyrd hruron,

to give gold in pay   for him who Grendel slew,
    criminally   as he would have killed others,
    unless mighty God   and that man's courage
had defended them   against that fate at last.
God governed all,   as yet he guides mankind.
    Therefore remember,   keep in mind ever,
forethought is best.   One will find here much
of both weal and woe   in his worlds journey,
        long lingering   in life's conflicts,
    Melody and music   mingled together
when before Halfdane's heir   the harper recited
    to murmuring strings   many a story,
and then Hrothgar's bard   raised excitement
along the meadbenches   as he made a song
how the hero Hnaef,   Halfdane leader,
    was to fall stricken   in a Fresian hall,
when the swift onslaught   sought out those people.
    Indeed Hildeburgh   need hardly praise
    faith of the Jutemen.   Faultless was she,
yet lost her loved ones   in lethal conflict;
    son an brother,   sorely wounded...

(MS Cotton Vitellius A XV f156)
Trans: Ruth P. M. Lehmann

Historical context

Warfare in the Anglo-Saxon period cannot be viewed as a uniform whole. The nature of warfare is a reflection of the society in which it takes place. Between the fifth and the ninth centuries Anglo-Saxon society evolved from a fragmented collection of tribes driven from their traditional homelands by the turmoil caused by the onslaught of the Huns and the collapse of the Roman empire, to a single state, able to withstand, and eventually repel, the ravagings of the Vikings.

When Atilla the Hun's hordes surged into western Europe they caused a wave of dislocation amongst the Germanic tribes. This, and a power vacuum in Britain following the withdrawal of the Imperial Roman administration, caused the migration. Bede records that the invaders came predominantly from three tribes the Angles, the Saxons and the Jutes.

The continental Germans were formed into large tribes held together, to a greater or lesser extent, by common language, laws and customs. As a consequence, when they fought they were able to muster sizeable armies. This degree of centralisation continued, possibly even increased, following the collapse of the Roman Empire, as the barbarian kings took over the existing administrations of the former provinces.

In contrast, in Britain the collapse of the Roman administration and the migration of the Germanic peoples precipitated a fragmentation of authority. The settlers who came to Britain do not appear to have come as tribes *en masse*, ruled by their hereditary royal houses. Rather, they came as small bands led by minor warlords. The first settlers are described as coming in just three ships, probably only about a hundred men. Any such details in early records must be treated with extreme caution, however, the small scale of the first migrations is repeatedly emphasised. Initially some of the settlers may have been invited, as the historical sources suggest, to bolster the defences against the Picts; they would not have been the first, there is evidence of Germanic troops stationed on Hadrian's Wall from as early as the third century, and by the time of the 'Barbarian Conspiracy' of AD 367 two of the principal 'Roman' commanders were in fact Germans.

The piecemeal nature of the migration led to the establishment of numerous minor kingdoms (**3**). The seventh-century Tribal Hidage, presumed to be a list of independent 'tribes' in the south of England liable to give tribute, possibly to Wulfhere of Mercia, lists 35 separate peoples. In addition, other kingdoms are known to have existed, both in the south of England and in the north, outside the suzerainty of Mercia. Gradually these kingdoms coalesced; the late sixth and seventh centuries are often known as the period of the 'heptarchy', a term first used by the historian Henry of Huntingdon in the twelfth century, reflecting the dominant position of the kingdoms of Wessex, Mercia, Northumbria, Kent, East Anglia, Essex and Sussex. Even then, within these kingdoms there were regions that were to a greater or lesser extent autonomous, ruled by minor kings and ealdormen.

Although histories such as the *Anglo-Saxon Chronicle* date the establishment of the major kingdoms to the late fifth and early sixth centuries, the first truly historical members of the ruling houses tend to date from the end of the sixth century. It is likely that it is closer to this time that the kingdoms were truly 'established' as regional powers.

Given the large numbers of Germanic troops serving in the Roman Army stationed in Britain and the propensity of Roman garrison forces to integrate with the local population the true date of the *Adventus Saxonum* must be considered to be much earlier than the date of AD 449 listed in the *Anglo-Saxon Chronicle*, or even the date of AD 380 listed by the Welsh historian Nennius. If the major kingdoms were only fully established at the end of the sixth century, it can be seen that the 'invasion' was not a decisive military expedition but a much more gradual rise to power spanning two centuries.

Before the establishment of the 'heptarchy' the majority of recorded battles were against the native population or 'welsh'. From the seventh century the focus changed to battles between the various Anglo-Saxon kingdoms. This division may to some extent be artificial however, since the establishment of the major kingdoms themselves from the various minor 'tribes' can hardly have been accomplished without conflict. The balance of power between the kingdoms shifted frequently; the venerable Bede, writing in AD 731, records seven kings who managed to achieve sufficient power to be able to force all the kingdoms south of the Humber to yield tribute and hence to claim the title *brytenwealda* or *bretwalda*, literally 'broad ruler' but later taken to mean 'ruler of Britain'. These bretwaldas were Ælle of the South Saxons (recorded in the *Anglo-Saxon Chronicle* as active between AD 477 and 491 but probably later), Ceawlin of the West Saxons (king AD 581-588), Æthelbert of Kent (died AD 616), Rædwald of the East Angles (died before AD 627), and three kings of Northumberland, Edwin (king AD 616-633), Oswald (king AD 634-642) and Oswiu (king AD 642-670). The claim that Edwin and Oswald held the title bretwalda may reflect Bede's Northumbrian bias, and certainly shows the limited nature of the office, since both were slain in separate battles with Penda, king of Mercia, before Penda was himself slain by Oswiu in AD 655.

Throughout the seventh century Northumbria and Mercia vied for hegemony over the southern kingdoms. Mercia eventually prevailed, while, or perhaps because, Northumbria spent most of the eighth century in a state of civil war between various rival claimants to the throne. The degree of authority Mercian kings exerted over the other southern kingdoms varied greatly. Kent appears at times to have been ruled directly by sub-kings of the Mercian royal family, while the *Anglo-Saxon Chronicle* records how the West Saxon king Cuthred fought many hard battles with Æthelbald, king of Mercia, during his 16 year reign, including defeating him at the battle of Beorford in AD 752.

All this was swept away by the arrival of the Vikings. Following seventy-six years of increasingly severe raids, beginning in AD 789, the 'Great Heathen Army' landed in East Anglia in AD 865. Ælla king of Northumberland was killed at York in

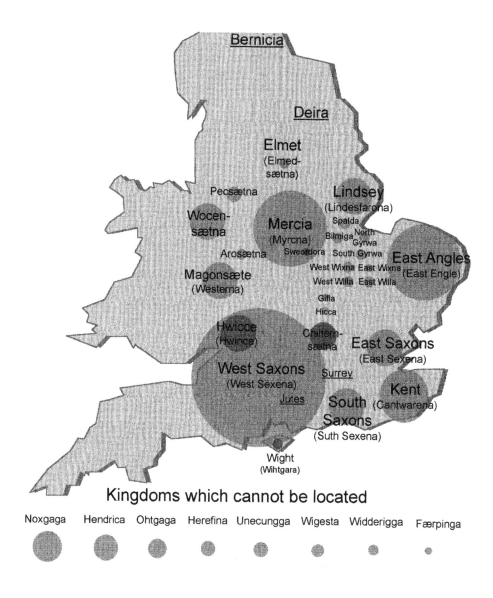

Bernicia

Deira

Elmet
(Elmed-
sætna)

Pecsætna

Lindsey
(Lindesfarona)

Wocen-
sætna

Mercia
(Myrcna)

Spalda

Bilmiga North
Gyrwa

Arosætna   Sweodora   South Gyrwa

East Angles
(East Engle)

West Wixna East Wixna
West Willa   East Willa

Magonsæte
(Westerna)

Gifla

Hicca

Hwicce
(Hwinca)

Chiltern-
sætna

East Saxons
(East Sexena)

West Saxons
(West Sexena)

Surrey

Jutes

South
Saxons
(Suth Sexena)

Kent (Cantwarena)

Wight
(Wihtgara)

Kingdoms which cannot be located

Noxgaga   Hendrica   Ohtgaga   Herefina   Unecungga   Wigesta   Widderigga   Færpinga

3   *Anglo-Saxon kingdoms listed in the seventh-century 'Tribal Hidage'. The 'size' of each kingdom is related to the number of hides listed in the Tribal Hidage and is not directly related to its actual size. The extremely large size of Wessex (100,000 hides) may well be a later amendment. The location of several of the kingdoms cannot be identified and several other kingdoms known from other sources (underlined) are also shown.*

AD 867 followed by Edmund king of East Anglia in AD 870. Mercia finally fell in AD 874, the king, Burhred, being forced to flee and Ceolwulf, a puppet of the Vikings, was set up in his place. Only Wessex, under the leadership of Alfred 'the Great', survived the storm.

2 Missile weapons

Hi leton þa of folman   feolhearde speru
grimme gegrundene   garas fleogan
bogan wæron bysige.

They let from their fists   filehard spears,
grimly ground   javelins flew,
bows were busy.
(*Battle of Maldon*, 108)

Before battle lines joined and warriors risked all, they would attempt to thin the enemy ranks with missiles. This would begin with archery, followed by an exchange of javelins and throwing axes immediately prior to the hand-to-hand combat.

The Javelin (including the Angon)

Gar, Daroð (dart)

ða he oþerne   ofstlice sceat,
ðæt seo byrne tobærst   he wæs on breostum wund
þurh ða hringlocan   him æt heortan stod
ætterne ord.

Then he hastily   shot the another man
so that his byrnie burst.   He was wounded in the chest
through the ring-locked shirt.   In his heart stood
the deadly point.
(*Battle of Maldon*, 143)

Spears were the most common weapon of the Anglo-Saxons, and were used both as missiles and as thrusting weapons for hand-to-hand combat (see Chapter 3). It is not generally possible to identify a spearhead as being specifically designed either as a missile or for hand-to-hand combat. Indeed, any spear might be used as a missile weapon *in extremis*, but it is usually assumed that shorter and lighter spears with smaller heads were preferred (**4**).

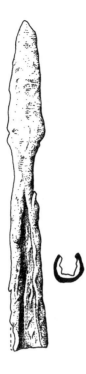

4 *Javelin head from Morning Thorpe, Norfolk, length 17.2cm. It is not generally possible to distinguish between javelins and spears designed for hand to hand combat, however, it is generally assumed that smaller and lighter spearheads would have been used for missiles.*

(Redrawn by K. R. Dixon)

The exception to this is barbed spears (**5**), commonly known as angons, which are known to have been missile weapons. These often have a long slender shank between the barbed point and the socket. They may have been derived from the Roman *pilum* although Roman authors describe them as a barbarian weapon. The Byzantine scholar Agathias recorded their use by Frankish warriors at the battle of Casilinum in AD 554:

> Suppose a Frank throws his angon in an engagement. If the spear strikes a man anywhere the point will penetrate, and neither the wounded man nor anyone else can easily pull it out because the barbs which pierce the flesh hold it in and cause terrible pain, so that even if the enemy is not fatally hit he still dies as a result. And if it sticks in the shield, it fixes in it at once and is carried around with it, the butt dragging on the ground. The man who has been hit cannot pull out the spear because the barbs have gone in, and he cannot cut it off because of the iron that covers the shaft. When the Frank sees this he quickly treads on it with his foot, stepping on the ferrule and forcing the shield downwards so that the man's hand is loosened and his head and breast bared. Then, taking him unprotected, he kills him easily either cleaving his head with an axe or piercing his throat with another spear.

5   *Barbed spear or angon from Abingdon, Berkshire, length 52.5cm. Angons were designed as missile weapons. The barbs would lodge in the opponent's shield so that it could not be removed and the iron shank prevented the head from being cut from the shaft.*

(Redrawn by K. R. Dixon after Swanton 1973)

Use

The maximum effective range of a javelin was probably in the region of 12-15m (40-50ft), depending on the length and weight of the javelin and the skill of the man throwing it.

The poem recording the battle at Maldon, Essex in AD 991 describes the encounter between the earl Byrhtnoth and a group of Vikings. The exchange begins when one of the Vikings throws a javelin at Byrhtnoth and wounds him, although he partially deflects it with his shield. Byrhtnoth then replies by throwing his two javelins, one at the Viking who had just wounded him, which hits him fatally in the neck, the second at another man, bursting through his mail byrnie and piercing his chest. A third Viking throws another javelin, again wounding Byrhtnoth. A young warrior with the earl pulls the javelin from the wound and throws it back, killing the man who threw it. Only after all this do the warriors draw their swords and engage each other in hand-to-hand combat.

The above passage highlights a common problem, that of having your own missile weapons used against you. *Grettir's Saga* describes an original, if unsuccessful, attempt to overcome this:

> He had a helmet on his head, a short sword by his side and a great spear in his hand without barbs and inlaid with silver at the socket. He sat down and knocked out the rivet that fastened the head in order to prevent Thorbjorn from returning the spear upon him.

> … Grettir went along the marsh and when he was within range launched his spear at Thorbjorn. The head was not so firm as he had intended it to be, so it got loose in its flight and fell off on to the ground.

The spear was traditionally associated with the god Woden/Odin and Viking sources indicate that casting a spear over (or at) an enemy was thought to bring about their doom. Thus Bede describes how, on his conversion to Christianity, the pagan priest Coifi cast a spear into his temple to defile it. A passage in *Eyrbyggja Saga* demonstrates that Odin's favour was not always ethereal:

> But as Snorri's company came up the scree, Steinthor cast a spear over Snorri's folk for his good luck, according to ancient custom; but the spear sought a mark for itself, and in its way was Mar, a kinsman of Snorri, who was straightway put out of the fight. When this was told to Snorri the Priest, he answered: 'It is well that men should see that he is not always in the best place that goes last.'

The Bow
Boga (Bow)

> *he wæs on Norðhymbron   heardes cynnes*
> *Ecglafes bearn   him wæs æscferð nama.*
> *He ne wandode na   æt þam wigplegan*
> *ac he fysde forð   flan genehe*
> *hwilon he on bord sceat   hwilon beorn tæsde*
> *æfre embe stunde   he sealde sume wunde*
> *þa hwile ðe he wæpna   wealdan moste.*

> He was a Northumbrian   of a hardy family,
> Ecglaf's son   Æscferth was his name.
> He never weakened   at the warplay,
> but sent forth   arrows swiftly.
> sometimes he shot a shield,   sometimes pierced a warrior
> time after time   he would wound someone,
> while-ever his weapon   he might wield.
> (*Battle of Maldon*, 266)

Finds of archery equipment are rare in England. A bow and arrows were found at Chessel Down on the Isle of Wight and traces of the wood of the bow stave on the soil are occasionally identified. Iron arrowheads survive more frequently and are found in about one percent of graves. It is often assumed that the scarcity of finds indicates that archery equipment was deposited in graves only infrequently, however, it should be recognised that neither bow staves nor arrows are likely to survive in English soil and the actual frequency with which they were deposited may have been much higher. Finds on the continent are somewhat more common; about forty bow staves and numerous arrows dating from the third or fourth century were found at Nydam,

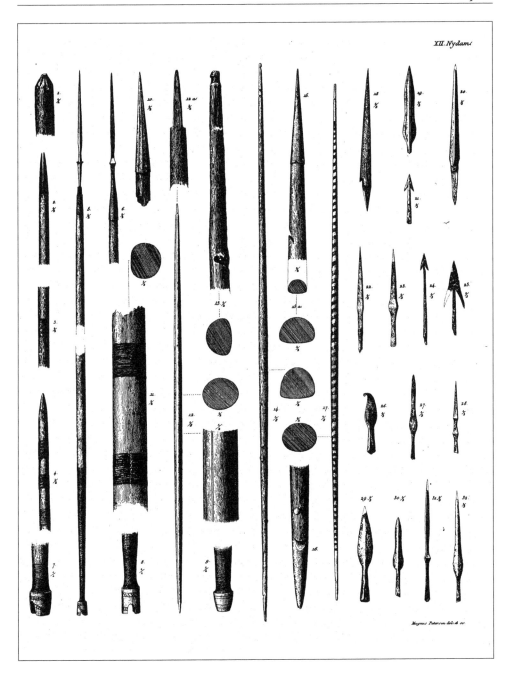

6   *Bows and other archery equipment from Nydam, Denmark. (Engelhardt)*

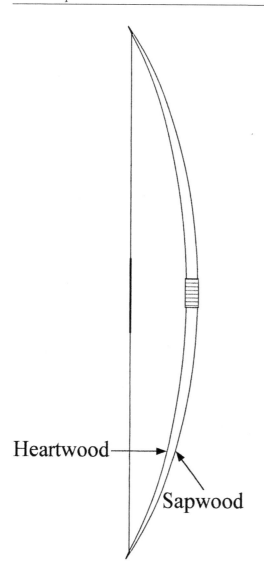

Heartwood

Sapwood

7 Schematic diagram of a longbow. The stave was traditionally made of yew with the back of the bow of sapwood and the belly of heartwood. In this way the stave formed a natural composite.

(Drawn by R. Underwood)

Denmark (**6**). Bows and arrows were also found at Thorsbjerg, Denmark and a Viking bow was found at Hedeby, Germany.

Germanic bows were 'longbows', that is they were made of a single piece of wood in contrast to Asiatic 'composite' bows. The bow stave of a longbow is carefully chosen so that the back of the bow is of sapwood and the belly is of heartwood (**7**). In this way the stave is a natural composite; the elastic sapwood works under tension, the resilient heartwood under compression. Traditionally yew is used, although ash and elm are also suitable. The string could be made of hair or animal gut.

The Nydam bows measured from 170-185cm (5ft 7in to 6ft) long and were mainly of yew. The bow staves were rounded rather than flat, forming a D-section in the centre and on one

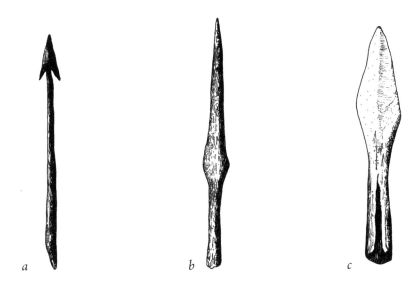

8　　*Anglo-Saxon arrowheads can be divided into three main types:*
a. Barbed head from Nydam, Denmark, length 9.1cm.
b. Square sectioned 'bodkin' from Nydam, Denmark, length 10.0cm.
c. Leaf shaped blade from West Stow, length 10.4cm.

(Redrawn by K. R. Dixon, a.,b. after Engelhardt, c. after West)

of the bows the ends of the stave, the nocks, were of horn. Horn bows, *hornbogan,* are also mentioned in *Beowulf.* Some of the staves were decorated with incised lines or had sections bound with thread. The Hedeby bow is also of yew, oval in cross-section and 192cm (6ft 3in) long.

Anglo-Saxon arrowheads can be divided into three main types (**8**). Leaf shaped arrowheads usually have a socket for attachment to the shaft. Triangular or square sectioned 'bodkins' and barbed arrowheads generally have a simple tang that was either driven into the end of the shaft or bound on. The size of arrowheads varies between 5.5cm (2in) and 15.5 cm (6in), and it is not always possible to distinguish between large arrowheads and small javelins (**9**).

Leaf-shaped and barbed arrowheads probably developed from hunting arrows and would have been most effective against unarmoured opponents. The late Roman writer Procopius described the difficulty of removing a Gothic barbed arrow from a face wound:

> One of the guards of Belesarius was hit by one of the Gothic archers between the nose and the right eye. And the point of the arrow penetrated as far as the neck behind, but it did not show through, and the rest of the shaft projected from his face and shook as the man rode.

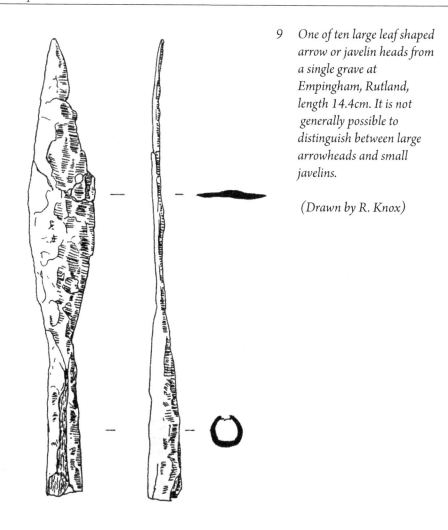

9   One of ten large leaf shaped
    arrow or javelin heads from
    a single grave at
    Empingham, Rutland,
    length 14.4cm. It is not
    generally possible to
    distinguish between large
    arrowheads and small
    javelins.

    (Drawn by R. Knox)

But afterwards one of the physicians, Theoctistus by name, pressed
on the back of his neck and asked weather he felt much pain. And
when the man said that he did feel pain he said, 'Then both you
yourself will be saved and you sight will not injured'. And he made
this declaration because he inferred that the barb of the weapon had
penetrated to a point not far from the skin. Accordingly he cut off
that part of the shaft which showed outside and threw it away, and
cutting open the skin at the back of the head, at the place where the
man felt the most pain, he easily drew towards him the barb, which
with its three sharp points now stuck out behind and brought with it
the remaining portion of the weapon.

10 *A number of Roman arrows with the fletchings surviving were found at Dura Europos, Syria. The shafts were painted red and black either to identify the owner or to mark a matching set. Similar marks were found on the arrow shafts from Nydam, Denmark.*

(Photograph from Rostovtzeff et al.)

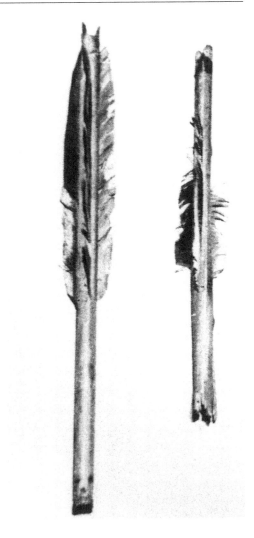

Conversely, bodkins appear to have been developed for use in battle against armoured opponents as the long tapering point could easily pass through the links of a mail shirt or even puncture the iron plate of a helmet if shot at close range.

The arrow-shafts from Nydam varied between 74cm and 94cm long (29-37in). They had been turned so that they tapered from the middle. The nock end, where the arrow was notched to take the bowstring, was broader than the shaft and the feather fletchings had been glued and bound in place with thread (**10**). Many of the shafts were marked with inscribed lines, probably to indicate matching sets. Later medieval treatises suggest ash was the best wood for arrow shafts although poplar was also commonly used. The shafts of the arrows from Chessel Down were of hazelwood.

Other archery equipment is extremely rare. A turned wooden quiver (**11**) and bronze fittings from a second were found at Nydam and a bone plate and fragments of leather, thought to be an archer's bracer, was found with other Anglo-Saxon artefacts at Lowbury

Hill, Berkshire (**12**). The function of the bracer was to protect the forearm from the bowstring during release (**13**).

Use

Bows appear to have been used more frequently in war than the grave evidence would suggest. They are referred to in literature and also depicted in art. One of the scenes on the eighth-century Northumbrian 'Franks' casket shows a single archer defending his hall against a group of warriors (**colour plate 4**). The name Egil appears in runes beneath the scene. Egil, brother of the mythical Weland Smith, was reputed to have been a master archer, although the tale that the scene depicts is not known.

The Bayeux tapestry shows no less than 29 archers, six in the main scene and 23 in the border (**14**). Only one is a Saxon, shown alongside the shieldwall as the other warriors hurl javelins at the Norman cavalry (see **72**). Several of the archers carry quivers, slung at either their waist or shoulder, and all but one are unarmoured. The intensity of their archery is illustrated by the number of arrows shown protruding from the shields of the Saxon warriors.

The maximum range of an Anglo-Saxon bow was probably in the region of 150-200m (500-650ft) although the effective range would be somewhat lower. Two factors are important: the accuracy of the shot and the momentum of the arrow when it hits the target. Ancient bows are typically accurate to a range of 50-60m (160-200ft). This would be the maximum range against individuals, although against formed bodies of men accuracy would be of less importance. At longer ranges the momentum of an arrow falls off

11 *Wooden quiver from Nydam, Denmark.*

(Photo courtesy Archäologisches Landesmuseum, Schleswig)

12   *Bone bracer from Lowbury, Berkshire, length 11cm. The bracer would have been tied to the inside of the forearm to protect it from the bowstring during release.*

(Drawn by K. R. Dixon)

13 *An archer preparing to shoot. He has a simple wooden longbow and an arrow with a leaf bladed head. The arrowhead is bound on with coloured thread which serves to identify it as one of a set. On his left arm he wears a bracer to protect his arm from the bowstring during release.*

14   *The Bayeux tapestry shows Norman archers supporting a cavalry attack on the Saxon shieldwall. Only one of the 29 archers shown on the tapestry wears mail and a helmet.*

(Drawn by K. R. Dixon)

rapidly due to air friction, at 50m (160ft) the penetration is only 75% of that at 10m (30ft). Therefore, at longer ranges, perhaps beyond 100-120m (325-400ft), arrows would cause only a few, if any, relatively minor wounds.

The effect of archery at close range is illustrated in *Njal's Saga*:

> After that Starkad egged on his men, and then they turn down upon them into the ness. Sigurd Swinehead came first and had a red shield, and in his other hand he held a sword. Gunnar saw him and shot an arrow at

him from his bow; he held the shield up aloft when he saw the arrow flying high, and the shaft passed through the shield and into his eye, and so came out at the nape of his neck, and that was the first man slain.

Most men would have learnt how to use a bow for hunting, since game would be an important supplement to the table, however, its use in war appears to have been limited to a few specialists. It is not clear why this is so, but it may be simply that to be effective an archer could not afford to be encumbered with the additional weapons with which to engage in hand-to-hand combat.

The Throwing Axe or Francisca
Æx, Æsc

Although generally associated with the Franks, with whom it is etymologically connected, the throwing axe or *francisca* was widely used by Germanic warriors and several examples have been found in England.

It is distinguished from the domestic hand axe (see Chapter 3) by the curved shape of the head. Two main forms can be distinguished, with either a convex or a 'S' shaped upper edge, although intermediate forms also occur (**15**).

Use

The Roman author Procopius, writing in the sixth century, described the Franks and their use of the throwing axes:

> … each man carried a sword and shield and an axe. Now the iron head of this weapon was thick and exceedingly sharp on both sides while the wooden handle was very short. And they are accustomed always to throw these axes at one signal in the first charge and thus shatter the shields of the enemy and kill the men.

The term francisca is now commonly accepted as referring to throwing axes, although contemporary sources use the term more widely. The sixth-century Frankish chronicler Gregory of Tours described the use of axes by Frankish warriors, but these are usually hand-axes:

> … *unus elevata manu bipennem cerebrum eius inlisit.*
> …one of the Franks raised his hand and struck his skull
> with his axe.
> (*History of the Franks* II.40)

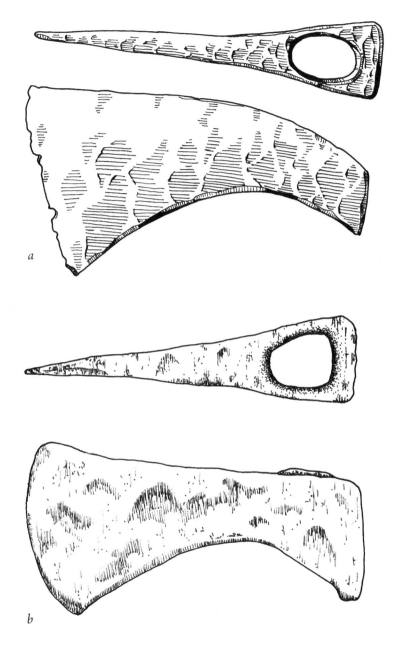

15 *Throwing axes or franciscas:*

a. *One of two franciscas from Burgh Castle, Norfolk with a convex upper surface (Redrawn by K. R. Dixon after Johnson 1983).*

b. *Francisca from Morning Thorpe, Norfolk with an 'S' shaped upper surface. (Redrawn by K. R. Dixon after Green et al.)*

Only once does he describe an axe being thrown:

> ... *proiecta secure paene cerebro eius inlisit. sed ille in parte excussus, ictum*
> *ferientis evasit.*
> ... threw an axe at him and nearly struck his skull. But he moved to one
> side, avoiding the blow.
> (*History of the Franks* IX.35)

Throughout his writings, Gregory of Tours uses two Latin terms for an axe, *securis* and *bipennis*. Isodore of Seville (AD 570-636), however, says that the Frankish axe was called a francisca, but does not make clear whether this term was used for a hand-axe or a throwing axe:

> *Secures ..., quas Hispani ab usu Francorum per derivationem Franciscas*
> *vocant.*
> Axes ..., which the Spanish because of their use by the Franks call
> Franciscas.
> (*Etymology*, XVIII.6.9)

Later writers, often paraphrasing Gregory of Tours, use the term francisca when describing the use of both hand axes and throwing axes.

The maximum effective range of a throwing axe is about 12m (40ft). Procopius makes it clear that the Franks threw their axes immediately before hand-to-hand combat. This would have the effect of disrupting the enemy line as well as possibly wounding or killing an enemy warrior.

The weight of the head and the length of the shaft allow the axe to be thrown with considerable momentum. As the axe tends to spin in flight the throw has to be carefully judged if the edge of the blade is to strike the target, although the weight of the head could cause injury in any event.

Sling
Liðere (Leather)

Evidence for the use of slings in war by the Anglo-Saxons is limited. The biography of Bishop Wilfred gives a description of the effective use of a sling to kill a pagan priest when the saint and his followers were attacked after their ship had run aground:

> Thereupon one of the companions of our bishop took a stone which
> had been blessed by all the people of God and hurled it from his sling
> (*de funda emittens*) after the manner of David. It pierced the wizard's
> forehead and penetrated to his brain as he stood cursing; death took
> him unawares as it did Goliath, and his lifeless body fell backwards on
> to the sand.

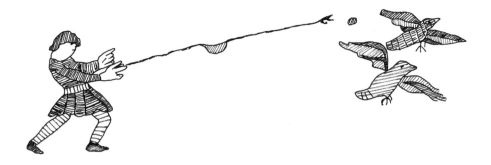

16   *A detail from the Bayeux Tapestry showing a man using a sling to hunt birds.*

(Drawn by K. R. Dixon)

However, it may be that the sling was not a weapon normally used in war. If we accept the passage at face value it can be argued that the sling was used more as a last resort than a weapon of choice. Furthermore, the proposition that Wilfred's biographer was more interested in making Biblical parallels than in recording the actual events cannot be dismissed. A man with a sling is shown hunting birds on the lower margin of the Bayeux tapestry (**16**).

3 Hand-to-hand combat weapons

us sceal ord and ecg   ær geseman

Between us point and edge   shall first decide ...
(*Battle of Maldon*, 60)

Two weapons defined the Anglo-Saxon social order, the spear and the sword. Slaves were denied the right to bear arms; consequently ownership of a spear defined a man as free and a warrior in Germanic society, while the cost and prestige of a sword marked its owner as a man of rank. Both the axe and the seax, the eponymous weapon of the Saxon, were primarily domestic implements and appear to have only rarely been employed as weapons.

The Spear
Spere, Ord (point), Æsc (ash), Sceaft (shaft), Gar

Forðon sceall gar wesan
monig morgenceald mundum bewunden
hæfan on handa

Henceforth shall spear be, on many cold morning,
grasped in fist, lifted in hand.
(*Beowulf*, 3021)

The spear was the primary weapon of the Anglo-Saxon warrior from kings and thegns down to the lowest ceorls. It is by far the most common weapon found, represented in around 85% of graves containing weapons or around 40% of adult male graves.
  A spear comprised an iron spearhead and a wooden shaft, traditionally of ash, although hazel, apple, oak and maple were also used. In addition, the butt end was sometimes protected with an iron ferrule.

The Spearhead

There is great diversity in the size and shape of spearheads. They have been categorised into four main groups, each with several sub-types.

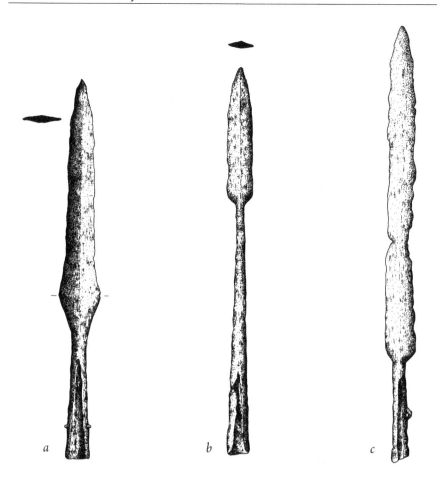

17   *Spearheads with angular blades:*
a.   *Curved edged, from Salisbury, Wiltshire. Note the remains of the attachment rivet and the wire inlay around the socket, Length 33.4cm.*
b.   *With long shank, from Prittlewell, Essex, Length 34.0cm.*
c.   *Sword-bladed, from Folkestone, Kent. Note the remains of the binding ring around the socket, Length 57.6cm.*

(Redrawn by K. R. Dixon after Swanton)

   By far the most common form of spearheads have angular blades, usually with a lozengiform (diamond) cross-section (**17** and **colour plate 3**). There is tremendous variety within the sub-groups: the most common form, dating to the late fifth and early sixth centuries, have concave curved edges, others have a long iron shank between the socket and the head, similar to the barbed angons (see below), while the most distinctive form have sword-like blades up to 50cm long. The length and weight of these sword-headed spears, together with the frequent reinforcement of the

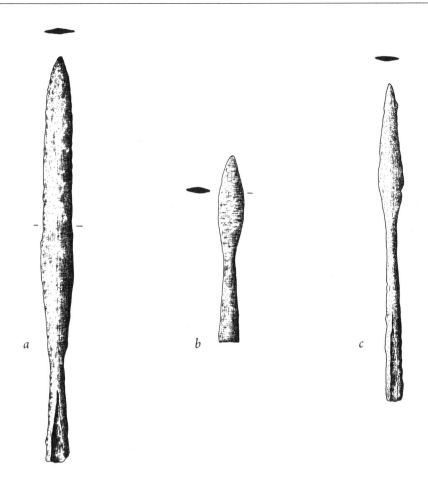

18   Spearheads with leaf shaped blades:
a.   Long blade, small socket, from Winterbourne Gunner, Wiltshire. Length 44.8cm.
b.   Small blade, small socket, from East Shefford, Berkshire. Length 16.4cm.
c.   Small blade, long socket, from Sarre, Kent. Length 42.9cm.

(Redrawn by K. R. Dixon after Swanton)

socket with a binding ring, suggests that they were wielded two handed using sideways cutting strokes rather than thrusts.

The second main group of spearheads have leaf shaped blades and are usually lentoid (lens-shaped) in cross-section. The various subgroups are distinguished by the relative proportions of the blade and the socket (**18**).

Two styles are clearly derived directly from earlier continental forms. The first are barbed spears, commonly known as angons. These often have a long slender shank between the barbed point and the socket. They are generally considered to have been missile weapons

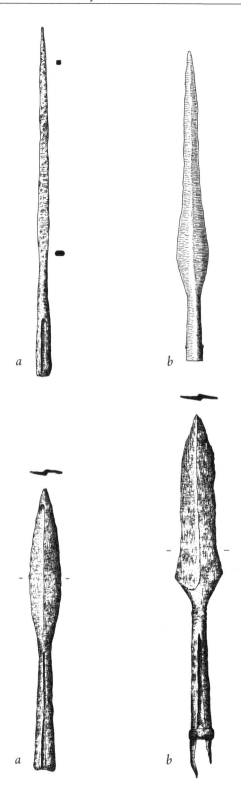

19 Spearheads based on a square cross section midrib:
a. Simple spike, from River Thames. Length 37.7cm.
b. With blade pieces welded to the midrib, from Fairford, Gloucestershire. Length 41.0cm.

(Redrawn by K. R. Dixon after Swanton)

20 Spearheads with corrugated blades:
a. Leaf shaped, from Barnes, Greater London. Length 30.1cm.
b. Angular, from Nassington, Northamptonshire. Length 38.2cm.

(Redrawn by K. R. Dixon after Swanton)

21 A spearhead from Buckland, Kent, decorated with fine wire inlay in the shape of a circle on one side of the blade and a swastika on the other.

(Redrawn by K. R. Dixon after Evison 1987)

(see Chapter 2). The second group have a midrib of square cross section (**19**). Some are simple spikes, others have thin blades welded to the midrib. Both forms would have been particularly effective in piercing the links of a mail byrnie.

In the last group of spearheads the blade is corrugated to increase the longitudinal strength of the blade without increasing the weight (**20**). This is a much simpler method of manufacture than mid-ribbing, which it appears to have replaced. Apart from their method of construction these spearheads otherwise resemble either the leaf shaped or angular blade forms.

Spearheads were occasionally decorated. Bronze and silver inlay was used to decorate both the blade and the socket. The most common blade ornamentation is a simple ring and dot motif, although more complex patterns were also used (**21**).

The socket was generally split along its length. This would allow the spearhead to be made firm on the shaft by hammering closed the socket onto the end of the shaft, which had been tapered to fit. The head was usually fixed to the shaft with one or occasionally two rivets that passed right through the socket. Occasionally an iron binding ring was fitted over the socket, strengthening the socket and giving an even firmer grip on the shaft.

The Ferrule

The butt of the spear was sometimes fitted with an iron ferrule, which usually took the form of a hollow cone that fitted over the tapering butt of the shaft (**22**). Much less common are ferrules with solid cones. These are formed with an iron spike, which is

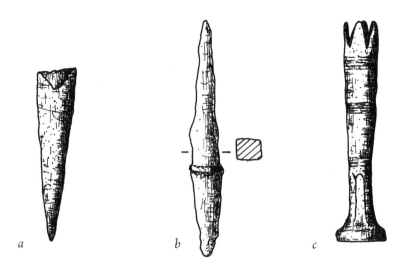

22   *Ferrules:*
        a. Simple hollow cone, from Pewsey, Wiltshire. Length 7.2cm.
        b. Solid with tang, from Buckland, Kent. Length 10.0cm.
        c. Unusual flat based ferrule decorated with incised lines, from Long Wittenhan,
        Berkshire. Length 9.2cm.

        (Redrawn by K. R. Dixon after, a. & c. Swanton, b. Evison)

hammered into the butt. Occasionally, the ferrule was decorated with metal inlay to match the spearhead.

The Shaft

Evidence for the length of spears is limited. It has been estimated from graves containing both a spearhead and butt-ferrule that they ranged in length from 1.6m to 2.8m (5ft 3in-9ft 3in); the shorter spears may have been used as missiles rather than in hand to hand fighting. This is significantly shorter than the complete continental examples found at Nydam which ranged from 2.3m to 3.0 m (7ft 8in - 10ft) long.

  The shaft may sometimes have been decorated, as were some of the shafts in the Danish finds. Iron and bronze rings were sometimes fitted onto the shaft and may have marked the centre of balance of the spear and thus the natural place to hold it. The shaft may also been painted.

23   *Alternative methods of using the spear:*

a.   *Overarm grip. With the spear held overarm, it must be gripped at the balance point. The high grip means that it can be more easily used against the opponent's face and upper body, and it can also be used more easily as a missile.*

b.   *Underarm grip. With the spear held underarm it is supported along the length of the forearm. This allows the shaft to be held behind the balance point, giving greater reach, and to be gripped more firmly, so that it can be used to parry enemy thrusts.*
      (Photographs: K.R. Dixon)

Use

Spears were usually wielded one handed with a shield held in the other hand. Evidence for exactly how they were employed is scarce. It appears that the spear could be gripped either underarm or overarm (**23**), shown on the Franks' Casket (**colour plate 4**) and the Bayeux Tapestry (see **72**), respectively. With an underarm grip the full length of the spear could be employed and greater force could be put into the blow. Overarm, the spear would have had to be gripped at the balance point, although blows could more easily be aimed over the enemy's shield at his face and shoulders.

Used one handed, the spear would have had limited use in single combat. To be effective ranks of spearmen stood together, forming a 'shieldwall'. This formation had several names, *scyldburh*, 'shield-fortress', *bordweal*, 'board-wall' and *wihagan*, 'war-hedge'. In this way they gained mutual protection from each other's shields while presenting a thicket of spearpoints to the enemy. It is generally assumed that the men stood close together, with the edges of their shields almost touching or even overlapping, often in a formation several ranks deep. In practice the thickness and depth of the shieldwall would probably have varied, depending on the size of the battlefield and the number of men involved (see Chapter 6).

Evidence for spears being used two handed is limited. An eighth-century stone relief from Aberlemno, Scotland (**24**) shows a Pictish warrior wielding a spear with both hands with his shield slung on a strap around his neck. The length and weight of some spearheads also suggests two-handed use, as noted above.

Although much later, a passage from *Grettir's Saga* describes the wound that a spear wielded in both hands could inflict:

> Then he went to the outer door and saw nobody there. It was raining hard, so he did not go outside, but stood holding both the doorposts with his hands and peering round. At that moment Thorbjorn sidled round to the front of the door and thrust his spear with both hands into Atli's middle, so that it pierced him through. Atli said when he received the thrust: 'These broad spear-blades are popular nowadays.'

24   *Detail from the Pictish eighth-century relief carved stone from Aberlemno, Scotland showing a warrior using a spear with both hands with his shield slung on a strap around his neck.*

(Drawn by K. R. Dixon)

The Sword
Sweord, Brond (brand), Mece, Secg, Bill, Heoru, Ecg (Edge)

... yrringa sloh
þæt hire wið halse heard grapode
banhringas bræc bil eal ðurhwod
fægne flæschoman

... angrily struck
so that it bit hard by the neck
the ribcage broke the sword passed straight through
the doomed body
(*Beowulf*, 1565)

The Blade

An Anglo-Saxon sword had a broad two-edged iron blade typically between 86cm and 94cm (34-37in) long (including the tang) and 4.5cm and 5.5cm wide (1¾–2¼in), although examples up to 100cm (40in) long or 6.5cm (2 ½in) wide have been found.

47

The method of manufacture of Anglo-Saxon sword-blades was a result of the poor quality of the iron available. Iron is made from iron ore by heating it in a reducing (oxygen free) environment in a furnace. In the Anglo-Saxon period the type of furnace used and the quality of the iron ore available meant that only small pieces of iron of variable quality could be produced. The furnace could not reach the high temperatures required to melt the iron into a homogeneous billet. Instead, the iron had to be forge welded from many small pieces into a single blade. Techniques for doing this had existed since the Iron Age. The iron was either beaten into thin sheets which were stacked together to form a laminated blade or formed into rods which were laid side by side and welded together.

Simple laminated and forge welded blades remained in use throughout the Anglo-Saxon period. The best swords, however, were made by a process known as pattern welding, in which the iron was beaten into strips that were then twisted together and forge welded. The twisting action tended to remove the surface slag that would otherwise cause weaknesses in the finished blade. A number of these twisted rods were then welded together side by side (**25**). Once the pattern-welded bar had been forged, strips of iron were welded onto each side to form the cutting edge, and the blade was ground to shape and polished.

The number of rods used and the direction of twist determined the surface pattern (**26**). Most typically three rods were used with the direction of twist alternating in adjacent rods, forming a herringbone pattern. Complex patterns could be formed with sections of straight and twisted rod (**colour plate 2**). If the above process was not complicated enough, the pattern-welded bars were sometimes used as part of laminated blades. Two thin pattern welded bars could be welded together or welded over a plain iron core (**27**).

Many swords had a fuller, a shallow groove that ran down the length of the blade, reducing the weight of the blade while maintaining the thickness. The fuller could be made by hammering or by removing some of the surface metal with a chisel. Hammering maintains the original herringbone pattern but if surface metal is removed the final pattern on the blade is formed of curves and resembles waves. Although both methods were used, hammering was much more common in England than on the continent.

The earliest pattern-welded swords date from the third century AD. It became increasingly popular through the fifth and sixth century and in the seventh century almost all blades were pattern-welded. After the seventh century its use declined as higher quality iron became available, although even in the tenth century around 45% of swords had pattern-welded blades.

The marks produced by pattern welding are frequently referred to in Anglo-Saxon verse. Terms such as *brogdenmæl* 'weaving marks' or *wundenmæl* 'winding marks' liken the pattern on the blade to the pattern in woven cloth. Other terms are *grægmæl* 'grey mark' and *scirmæled* 'brightly patterned', while *hringmæl* 'ring mark' or 'ring decoration' may refer to the pattern on the blade or to the decoration of the hilt with a 'sword ring' (see below). The process by which the pattern was produced is also alluded to

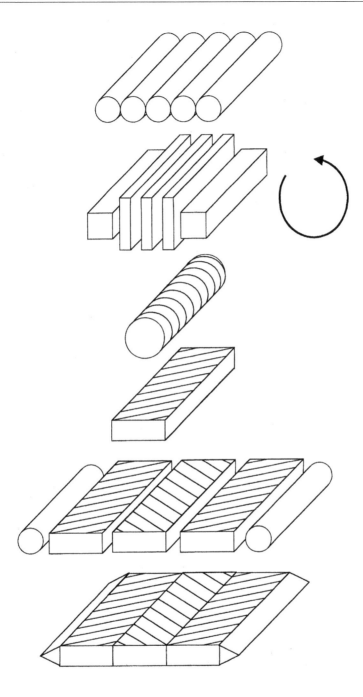

25   *Pattern welding method. Five rods of iron are formed into square or rectangular bars and welded together. The composite bar is then twisted and beaten flat. Three such bars form the core of the blade while two more iron rods welded to the core are ground down to form the cutting edges.*
(Drawn by R. Underwood)

Two rods	Three rods	Four rods

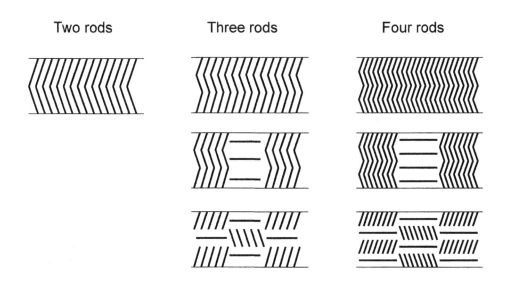

26   *Patterns formed by the pattern welding process. The basic pattern is determined by the number of rods used. More complex patterns can be produced by alternating twisted and straight sections of rod.*

(Drawn by R. Underwood)

in the phrase *fyrmælum fag* 'gleaming with the marks of the fire'. Other allusions to the method of manufacture of sword blades are also made. The blade was hardened by quenching, rapidly cooling the blade from red heat by immersing it in oil or water, so swords are described as *ahyrded heaþoswate* 'hardened by blood of battle'. Similarly, the working of the blade is evoked by descriptions of swords as *hamora lafum*, 'hammered blades' and the grinding to take an edge by *fela laf frecne* 'the terrible survivor of files' or *mecum mylenscearpum*, 'blades grindstone-sharp'.

The sides of the blade ran parallel from the hilt until close to the point. As a consequence the centre of balance was roughly halfway down the blade. This would make the sword good for hacking strokes but more difficult to use for thrusting. By contrast the blades of Anglo-Viking swords in the ninth and tenth centuries tapered inwards from the hilt to the point. This, together with the greater weight of the metal hilt, gave a centre of balance much closer to the hilt, so that the sword was better balanced for thrusting and parrying.

The sword blade terminated in a narrow strip of iron 11cm to 12cm long, known as the tang, over which the hilt was fitted.

The Hilt

The hilt was made in three parts, the lower guard, the grip and the upper guard. Pre-Viking swords had hilts made largely of perishable materials such as wood, horn or bone which

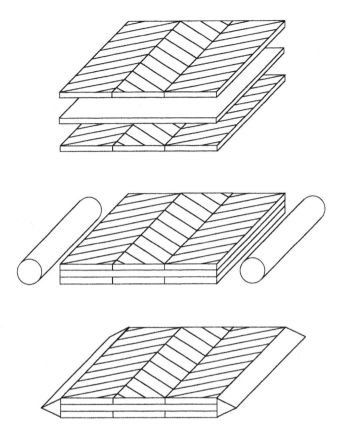

27 *Construction of a laminated blade. Two pattern-welded bars are forged together over a soft iron core and hard iron edges are attached and ground to shape.*

(Drawn by R. Underwood)

rarely survive, although they were often decorated with metal fittings. The basic construction of sword hilts changed little from the fifth to the eighth century, although metal decorative fittings are more frequent on later swords. The style of decoration also developed, reflecting the contemporary styles of decorative metalwork. The style and construction of sword hilts underwent significant change in the late eighth and ninth centuries. Later sword hilts were made largely of iron and derive from a quite separate Viking tradition of sword manufacture.

The three sections of the hilt fitted over the tang, the end of which was hammered out, often over an iron bar or washer, to hold them in place (**28**). The lower and upper guards were lentoid, typically between 7cm and 9cm wide and 2cm deep. The lower guard therefore only extended about 2cm on either side of the blade and would provide limited protection to the hand.

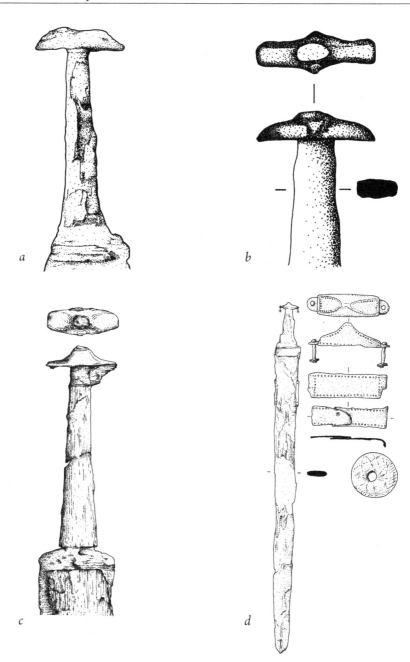

28   Pommel forms:
      a. Simple iron pommel, from Buckland, Kent.
      b. Early form, from Smelston, Sussex.
      c. Cocked hat — pierced by tang, from Morning Thorpe, Norfolk.
      d. Cocked hat — decorative, from Westgarth Gardens, Suffolk.
      (Redrawn by K. R. Dixon after, a. & b. Evison, c. Green et al., d. West)

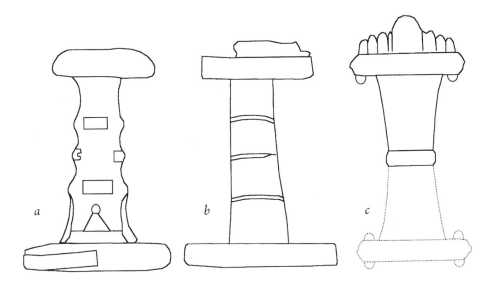

29 *Three forms of sword grip:*
a. *Circular or oval cross-section with grooves for the fingers. This style was in use from the earliest times and is similar to the grips on Roman spathae. (Cumberland Hilt. Seventh century).*
b. *Elongated hexagonal cross-section. Instead of grooves, the spacing of the fingers is marked with incised lines (Frankish sword hilt from Childeric's tomb. Fifth century).*
c. *Oval cross-section with sides curving outwards from the middle of the grip. (Fetter Lane hilt. Eighth century).*

(Drawn by K. R. Dixon)

Although evidence for the shape of the grip is extremely limited at least three distinct forms can be identified (**29**). The first is circular or oval in cross-section, the sides roughly parallel, with four deep grooves running round in which the fingers lie when the sword is gripped. This style was in use from the earliest times and is similar to the grips on Roman *spathae*. This form of grip can be seen on the Cumberland hilt (**colour plate 6**) and on early continental swords such as those from Nydam, Denmark. The second style has an elongated hexagonal cross-section, with sides parallel or tapering inwards slightly from lower to upper guard. Instead of grooves, the spacing of the fingers is marked with incised lines. On the continent, these grips were covered with gold foil and numerous complete examples of this type have been found. Although they are not found in England, a wire ring found on a sword hilt from Buckland, Kent showed that it had a grip with a hexagonal cross-section. The third form has a simple oval cross-section with sides either parallel or curving outwards from the middle of the grip.

The grips were generally surprisingly short, generally being between 7.5cm and 10cm long

(3-4in). The shortest grips could not fit the full width of an adult man's hand and must have been held either with the upper guard and pommel resting in the palm of the hand or with the index finger extended over the lower guard.

The most common form of decorative metal fitting was a 'pommel' of silver or bronze attached to the upper guard. Occasionally the pommel was functional in that the tang passed through the pommel where it was riveted on the top to fix the hilt in place, but usually it was purely a decorative feature that hid the end of the tang (**28d**). The earliest form has a rounded top and four-cornered base, while the most common form is pyramidical in shape, known as a 'cocked hat' pommel. In addition to the pommel, either or both of the guards could be decorated with a metal plate on their upper or lower surface (**30**). These plates were attached to the guard using decorative rivets with exaggerated heads. As well as being decorative these plates would serve to protect the wooden guard from wear. The grip was also occasionally decorated with metal fittings, such as at Sutton Hoo (**colour plate 5**) or the Cumberland hilt (**colour plate 6**).

A few swords bear runic inscriptions, such as the sixth-century sword from Gilton, Kent (**31**), which on one side bears an inscription:

This has been translated as:

EIC SIGIMER NEMDE
Sigimer named this sword

Five faint runes are barely discernible on the other side of the pommel. These cannot be deciphered but may record the name of the sword.

The tradition of naming swords is well attested in Anglo-Saxon verse. Perhaps the most famous such sword was *Hrunting* which was given to the hero Beowulf before he entered the lake to slay Grendel's mother:

> This sword which Hrothgar's aid lent to Beowulf in his need was by no
> means the least of powerful allies. That blade bore the name of Hrunting;
> it was among the foremost of ancient treasures. Its edged blade was of
> iron, gleaming with venom and hardened in the blood of battle; never
> had it failed any man who had grasped it in battle.

When this sword failed to have any effect on the ogress, Beowulf used a second sword that he found beneath the lake. This sword bore the name of the warrior for whom it was first made, exactly as did the Gilton sword:

> Likewise also on the hilt of bright gold, in runic symbols rightly

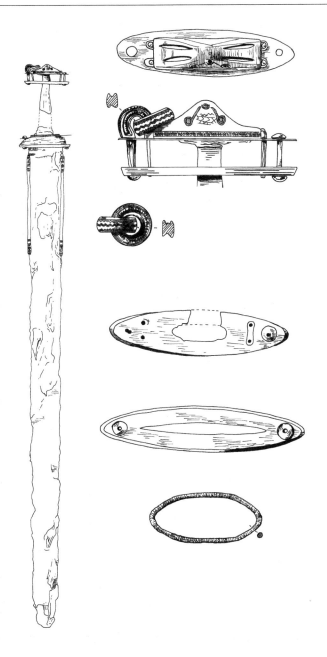

30 *Sword hilt from Buckland, Kent. The hilt was ornamented with silver plates riveted to the upper and lower guards and a silver pommel and sword ring with niello decoration. Niello is produced by the application of silver salts (particularly silver sulphide) onto the metal surface, followed by heating. The salts oxidise, leaving a black residue of silver oxide. There are traces of cord binding round the neck of the scabbard.*

(Redrawn by K.R. Dixon after Evison 1987)

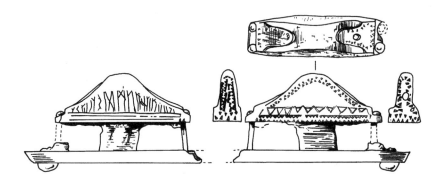

31   *Inscribed pommel from Gilton, Kent dated to around AD 550. The inscription can*
        be translated as 'Sigimer named this sword'. Five faint, indecipherable runes on the
        reverse of the pommel may have indicated the name of the sword.

        (Drawn by K. R. Dixon)

inscribed, was set down and recorded for whom that sword, noblest of blades, was first made, with its hilt of twisted work and its serpentine colours.

In the sixth century hilts often had rings attached to the upper guard adjacent to the pommel (**30** and **colour plate 9**). The earliest of these 'sword-rings' consisted of a fixed ring-staple attached to the upper guard to which a second free-running ring was linked. Both rings are usually decorated with bands of ornament.

It has been suggested that the ring may have been used to attach a cord or thong so that the sword could be attached to the wrist so as to keep the hand free while allowing the sword to be quickly brought to hand when required. This practice is mentioned several times in Viking sagas, such as that of Egil Skallagrimsson:

> ... when he saw where Berg-Onund was, he drew his sword; and there
> was a cord on the hilt, and he slipped it onto his arm and let it hang there.
> He took a spear in his hand ...

The cord could also have been used to fasten the sword into the scabbard to prevent it being drawn (see below).

Alternatively the presence of a ring may have been symbolic. Later hilts were decorated with a solid knob cast in the form of a pair of interlocking rings (**32**). These ring knobs clearly recall the earlier free-running rings yet cannot have served any practical purpose

32   *Sword from Sarre, Kent with silver sword-ring. The ring is fused to the staple rather than being free running. This is presumably a later development and is more common on the continent than in England.*

(Redrawn by K.R. Dixon after Evison)

and must therefore have been either decorative or symbolic. A number of swords have been found where the asymmetrical shape of the pommel suggests a sword ring was attached but had been removed in antiquity, perhaps because the sword ring was associated with a particular owner and removed if it passed to another, or that it was removed prior to burial.

There are frequent references to the giving of rings by a lord to his warriors in Anglo-Saxon poetry. In the poem *Widsið* the eponymous poet mentions a ring given to him by Eormanric, king of the Goths, worth six hundred shillings. A number of synonyms refer to the practice, such as *beag-gifa* 'ring-giver' and hence 'lord' and *hringsele* 'ring-hall'. These rings are generally assumed to have been finger or arm rings but they could equally have been rings to be fitted to a sword, particularly since jewellery is rarely found in male graves.

Both the ring and the sword hilt were particularly associated with the taking of oaths. The Danish chronicler Saxo says how:

> ... in old times those who were about to put themselves in dependence of
> the king used to promise fealty by touching the hilt of the sword.

The attachment of a ring to the hilt of the sword would, therefore, have been doubly symbolic and would have served to reinforce the seriousness of the oath. Often the sword on which the oath of fealty was sworn was given to the swearer. The acceptance of a sword was thus a symbol of client status. The presence of a ring on the hilt of a sword may therefore have indicated the status of the bearer was either one who received oaths of fealty or one who had given such an oath.

Swords of the pre-Christian period can usually be dated from their associated grave assemblages, and occasional finds of directly datable objects, particularly coins. The earliest swords tend to be without any metal fittings on the hilt, although such swords are known in all periods. It is sometimes assumed that some swords were stripped of their fittings prior to being placed in the grave, although such a thesis clearly cannot be proved.

Although the earliest swords reflected the contemporary continental tradition, English swords rapidly developed an insular style, indicating local manufacture, and several forms of hilt that developed on the continent in the seventh and eighth century are not found in England. While some movement of swords, in trade or otherwise, clearly took place in the sixth century, the distribution of certain styles of fittings suggest that the export of swords from England was as common, if not more so, than importation.

Swords of the early sixth century typically had a few simply decorated fittings: a bronze, sometimes silvered, pommel with perhaps guard plates on either the upper or lower guard only. In the late sixth and seventh century the fittings were more likely to be of silver, sometimes gilded, and full sets of both upper and lower guard plates and a pommel are more common. These pommels are often decorated with stamped patterns, incised lines or niello (**30**). The finest swords had hilts decorated with gold and cloisonné work. Several examples have been found on the continent but they are extremely rare in England, the most notable example coming from Sutton Hoo (**colour plate 5**).

From the mid seventh century onwards the dating of swords becomes more problematic as they are no longer found in graves in association with other more datable objects, rather they tend to be chance finds often recovered from river beds. Dating therefore is usually done by comparison of the style of ornament with wider trends in decorative metalwork. This generally precludes the dating of undecorated finds.

Sword hilts decorated with silver-gilt or gold plates with filigree decoration (**colour plates 7 and 8**) are dated to the eighth century and as such probably represent the last examples of truly Anglo-Saxon swords. Later swords owe far more to a quite separate development of the Germanic longsword that had been occurring in Scandinavia, brought to England by the Vikings.

The Scabbard

A sword was kept in a scabbard both to protect the owner from the blade and to protect the blade from the environment. It was generally made of wood and often covered with leather. The inside of the scabbard was frequently lined with fleece or fur, which may have acted as a reservoir for oil or grease which would serve to eliminate moisture and so protect the blade from rust.

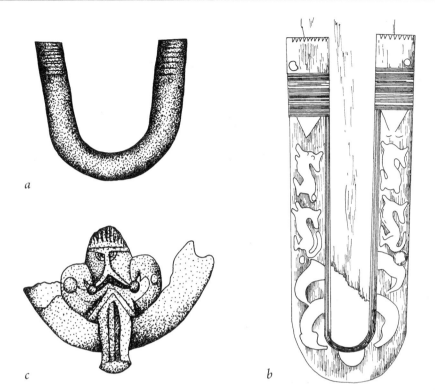

33   The bottom of the scabbard was sometimes protected from wear by a metal chape:
      a. Simple chape from Little Wilbraham, Cambridgeshire.
      b. Chape with niello decoration from Brighthampton, Oxfordshire.
      c. Chape with cast decorative figure from Abingdon, Berkshire.

      (Redrawn by K. R. Dixon after Menghin)

  The neck of the scabbard was sometimes protected against wear with a metal binding. The simplest bindings are no more than a strip of bronze wrapped around the neck, sometimes secured with a single rivet and decorated, if at all, with a simple pattern of punched dots or incised lines (**28d**). Others were cast, allowing more elaborate decoration (**colour plate 11**). Where the neck was not fitted with a metal binding it was sometimes protected by thong, twine or woven braid wrapped around the neck (**30**).

  The end of the scabbard might also be protected from wear by a chape (**33**). This was generally made of bronze or silver in a simple U shape and decorated with incised lines. Occasionally the chape was more highly decorated with niello or with cast features.

  The sword was suspended from either the waist, on a belt, or the shoulder, on a baldric, on the 'natural' side, i.e. left hip for a right handed man, to allow the long blade to be drawn across the body.

  The majority of swords show no evidence of fittings to attach the scabbard to the belt or

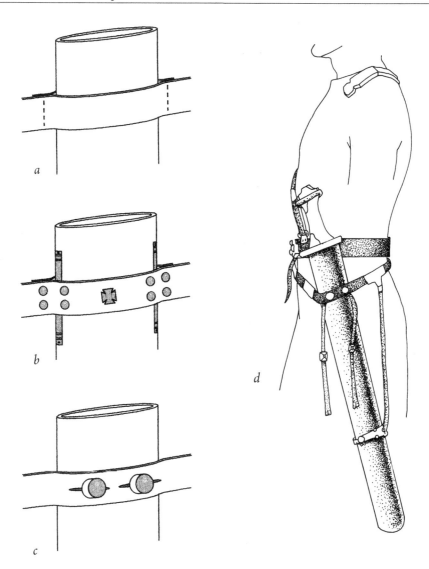

34   Suspension of the sword:
a.   Possible method of suspension of a scabbard with no fittings.
b.   Scabbard with reinforcing strips and decorative rivets from Brighthampton,
        Oxfordshire.
c.   Scabbard with decorative buttons and 'white' beads The difficulty with this method of
        suspension is that the sword does not hang freely with the centre of gravity directly
        below the point of suspension, instead the hilt pulls into the body and the tip of the
        sword hangs outwards. This does not occur when the scabbard is suspended from both
        front and back.
d.   Reconstruction of the method of suspension of the sword from Sutton Hoo, Suffolk,
        with a second attachment point near the tip of the sword.
        (a.-c. drawn by R. Underwood, d. redrawn by K. R. Dixon after Bruce-Mitford)

baldric and it may simply have passed through a loop sewn in the belt (**34**). This method would be most effective if the scabbard tapered, even if only slightly, along its length. Occasionally scabbards had strips of bronze or silver on either side, extending down from the neck between 6cm and 15cm, which would reinforce the scabbard for this form of suspension. Sometimes these reinforcing strips are accompanied by decorative rivets that serve either to attach the belt to the scabbard or to form the loop through which the scabbard passed.

An alternative method of suspending the sword is clearly shown on the helmet plates from Vendel, Sweden (**47**). The baldric is split at intervals along its length and two buttons, attached to the scabbard, pass through the slits. Two metal buttons, decorated with gold and garnets, were found in association with the sword at Sutton Hoo. They had been mounted in beads of a white material, possibly bone or ivory. Since the upper part of the scabbard was bound with fine linen tape, the buttons were presumably sewn on to the tape.

Some scabbards had a second attachment point further down the blade, as well as the main suspension point close to the neck. A strap ran from the lower half of the blade to the waist belt. This second strap would lift the tip of the sword and prevent it from swinging when the wearer moved.

A single bead of glass or amber was occasionally attached to the neck of the scabbard with a strap or thong. The function of the bead is not known. It may have served as an amulet; two Icelandic sagas, *Cormac's Saga* and *Laxdæla Saga*, refer to swords with associated 'healing stones' which could be used to heal wounds inflicted by the sword, although these stones were kept in bags, either tied to the scabbard or worn around the neck. Alternatively, the bead and thong may have had the much more mundane function of securing the sword in the scabbard. A passage in *Gisli's Saga* refers to *friðbond* 'peace-bands' with this function; the two sons of Vesteinn set out to kill Thorkell in revenge for their father's death:

> The elder said 'Who is that most distinguished man sitting near us? I have never seen a handsomer and nobler-looking person.' 'I am obliged to you for your words,' said he; 'I am called Thorkell.' The boy said 'That sword that you are holding in your hand must be a fine treasure. I wonder if you would let me see it?' Thorkell replied 'That is an odd thing to ask. Still I will show it to you all the same,' and he passed it to him. The boy took the sword and turned slightly and unfastened the peace-bands and drew the sword. And when Thorkell saw this, he said 'I never gave you leave to draw the sword.' 'I did not ask you for leave,' said the boy, and he raised the sword and struck at Thorkell's neck with it, so that it cut off his head.

Garnet-inlayed pyramids, either singly or more usually in pairs, are occasionally found in association with swords, both in England and on the continent. Their position relative to the sword varies, making the interpretation of their function difficult. Sometimes they

35 *A warrior using a sword and shield from the Bayeux tapestry. The sword is held with the arm almost straight to give power to the heavy cutting stroke. The shield is held out away from the body to increase the protection it affords.*

(Drawn by K. R Dixon)

are found on or by the sword in a similar position to the metal buttons described above, and therefore presumably were part of the suspension mechanism. At other times they are found some distance from the sword, implying they were suspended on straps or thongs in a similar manner to sword beads.

Use

The weight and balance of Anglo-Saxon swords suggests that they were mainly used for heavy cutting strokes rather than thrusting (**35**). This is confirmed by literary descriptions of combat which emphasise the weight of the blows landed:

> *Gehyrde ic þæt Eadweard anne sloge*
> *swiðe mid his swurde swenges ne wyrnde*
> *þæt him at fotum feoll fæge cempa*

> I heard that Edward struck one
> so fiercely with his sword the swing not withheld
> that he fell at his feet the doomed warrior.
> *(Battle of Maldon,*117)

*36   The main blows
with a sword were
to the head or shoulders, to
the left leg, below the
shield,and to the
sword arm.*

Anglo-Saxon sources, however, rarely have sufficient detail to give insight into exactly how the sword was used. The Viking sagas, although composed much later, provide a much more vivid picture.

Three main strokes appear to have been made, to the head, either downwards to land on the head or shoulders, or sideways aimed at the neck, both clearly intended as killing blows; to the lower (left) leg, below the shield; to the sword arm (**36**). The following descriptions of combat show the damage these blows could inflict:

> Then Thorbjorn rushed upon Grettir and struck at him, but he parried it with the buckler in his left hand and struck with his sword a blow which severed Thorbjorn's shield in two and went into his head, reaching the brain. (*Grettir's Saga*)

> Then he turned upon Gunnar himself and struck a blow that severed his shield right across below the handle, and the sword struck his leg below the knee. Then with another rapid blow he killed him. (*Grettir's Saga*)

37 A typical sequence of blows in a duel between two swordsmen:

a. The warriors face each other in a 'ready' stance. The left leg is forward and weight is evenly distributed on both feet. The sword is held up ready to strike and the shield is held out away from the body, giving maximum coverage.

b. The warrior on the left shifts his weight onto his left foot and steps forward with his right to makes a cut to his opponent's head. The opponent raises his shield to parry the blow.

c. The warrior on the left avoids the parry and brings his sword down to hit his opponent on the left thigh, below the shield.

(Photographs: K.R. Dixon)

... then he drew his sword and smote at Modolf; but Modolf made a cut at him too, and Kari's sword fell on Modolf's hilt, and glanced off it on to Modolf's wrist, and took the arm off, and down it fell, and the sword too. (*Njal's Saga*)

The effect of such grievous wounds was not always fatal however, as the tale of Onund Treefoot in *Grettir's Saga* shows. Onund was preparing to board an enemy ship in a sea battle:

Onund was stepping out with one foot on to the bulwark, and as he was striking they made a thrust at him with a spear; in parrying it he bent backwards, and at that moment a man on the forecastle of the king's ship struck him and took off his leg below the knee, disabling him at a blow.

Despite his wound Onund recovered and went about for the rest of his life with a wooden leg, hence his nickname Onund Treefoot. His disability did not prevent him continuing to have an active life, in a subsequent sea-battle:

[His companions] shoved a log under the stump of his leg, so that he stood pretty firm. The Viking (Vigbjod) dashed forward, reached Onund and hewed at him with his sword, which cut right through his shield and into the log beneath his leg, where it remained fixed. As Vigbjod bent down to pull his sword clear again, Onund dealt him a blow on his shoulder, severing his arm and disabling him.

Vigbjod was not as fortunate as Onund and died of his wound.

That the violence of these passages is not exaggerated is borne out by the archaeological evidence of weapon injuries on the skeletal remains of the dead. In a recent survey of six skeletons from the Anglo-Saxon cemetery at Eccles, Kent, all of which showed evidence of weapon injuries, three bore single long sword-cuts to the left-hand side of the skull. The rest had multiple injuries, one had been hit three times, again on the left hand side of the skull; the second had been hit in the spine by a projectile, either an arrow or a javelin, which probably disabled him followed by a single sword-cut to the head; the third had suffered a particularly brutal death with evidence of at least eighteen separate sword-cuts. There were a minimum of seven blows to the head, three to the arms and eight to the back. The cuts to the arms would have severed the muscles, preventing him from making any effective resistance. This was then followed by the blows to the head and back that must certainly have been fatal. Indeed on all the victims the blows to the head would have been incapacitating, if not immediately fatal.

38 An alternative sequence
    of blows:
a. *The warriors face each
    other in a 'ready'
    stance.*

b. *The warrior on the left
    steps forward and
    makes a cut to his
    opponent's head.*

c. *The warrior on the
    right counters the blow
    by hitting his opponent
    on the right forearm.*

    *(Photographs:
    K.R.Dixon)*

It should be remembered that the injuries listed above represent only those that were deep enough to damage the bone. The victims may have suffered other soft tissue injuries, particularly piercing blows, for example from spear thrusts.

Heavy blows were necessary to ensure they were immediately disabling if not fatal, otherwise the opponent might have chance to return the blow:

> Next Helgi leapt so boldly out of the door so that those nearest shrunk aback. Thorgils was standing near, and struck after him with a sword, and caught him on the shoulder and made a great wound. Helgi turned to meet him, and had a wood-axe in his hand, and said, 'Still the old one will dare to look at and face weapons,' and therewith he flung the axe at Thorgils, and the axe struck his foot, and a great wound that was. (*Njal's Saga*)

This is not to say that it was just strength, not skill, which was important. Heavy blows made without care could lead to the sword being lost or damaged:

> Sigmund drew his sword and cut at Skarphedinn, and the sword cut into his shield, so that it stuck fast. Skarphedinn gave the shield such a quick twist that Sigmund let go his sword. (*Njal's Saga*)

> Thorbjorn Angle took his sword in both hands and hewed at Grettir's head. So mighty was the blow that the sword could not hold against it, and a piece was broken out of the edge. (*Grettir's Saga*)

In such circumstances the quality of the blade was important. Swords often appear to have become blunt or to have been bent in the thick of combat:

> So then they set to. Cormac's sword bit not at all, and for a long while they smote strokes one upon the other, but neither sword bit. At last Cormac smote upon Thorvard's side so great a blow that his ribs gave way and were broken … (*Cormac's Saga*)

> So then befell a great battle, and Steinthor was at the head of his own folk, and smote on either hand of him; but the fair-wrought sword bit not when it came against a shield, and often he had to straighten it out under his foot. (*Eyrbyggja Saga*)

The Seax
Seax

þa gen sylf cyning …
…wællseaxe gebræd
biter ond beaduscearp   þæt he on byrnan wæg

Then the king himself …
…drew the slaughter-seax
bitter and battle-sharp   that he wore on his byrnie.
(*Beowulf*, 2702)

Seax is the Anglo-Saxon word used to describe both a single edged knife, with a blade length between 8cm to 31cm in length, i.e. akin to anything from a small camping-knife to a large cooks knife, and a 'long-seax' or single edged sword with a blade length ranging from 54cm to 76cm i.e. similar to a machete (**39**). The term 'scramasax' is also often used although it occurs only once in a historical account, in the *History of the Franks* by Gregory of Tours. He describes how the sixth-century Frankish king Sigibert is assassinated by two young men using 'strong knives commonly called scramasaxes' (*cultris validis quos vulgo scramasaxos vocant*). It should be noted that, given the date, the reference was probably to large knives rather than long-seaxes.

Knives are classified according to the shape of the blade and six main types have been identified (**40**). The most numerous style, with both the back and the cutting edge curving

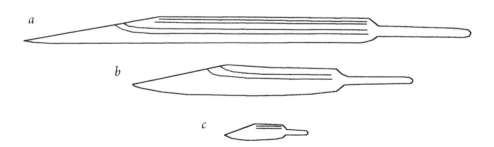

39   *Seaxes:*
a.   *Longseax from the River Thames at Battersea, length 72cm.*
b.   *Seax or knife from the River Thames at Wandsworth, length 45cm.*
c.   *Seax or knife (Museum of London), length 14cm.*

(Redrawn by R. Underwood after Gale)

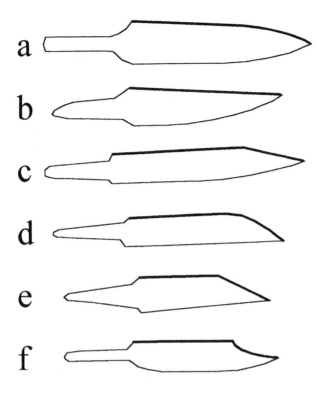

40 *Knife types:*
a. *Curved back, curved cutting edge, late fifth to early eighth century.*
b. *Straight back, curved cutting edge, late fifth to late seventh century.*
c. *Angled back, curved cutting edge, mid sixth to early eighth century.*
d. *Curved back, straight cutting edge, early seventh to early eighth century.*
e. *Angled back, straight cutting edge, late sixth to early eighth century.*
f. *Straight back in-curved near tip, curved cutting edge, late seventh century.*

(Redrawn by R. Underwood after Evison)

to the point, remained in use from the fifth century at least until the end of the pagan period and probably beyond. Other styles developed throughout the period. Seaxes have also been classified depending on how narrow or broad the blade is in relation to its length.

The blade of the knife terminates in an iron tang by which the grip was attached. The grip was made of perishable material such as wood, horn or bone, and does not generally survive. The majority of knives have quite short tangs, between 3cm and 7cm (1-3in) long, although occasionally it is much longer, suggesting the grip was suitable to be gripped in two hands (**41**). The tang is usually a plain iron bar tapering towards the end. It can therefore be presumed that the grip was bored out to hold the tang which was held in place by friction,

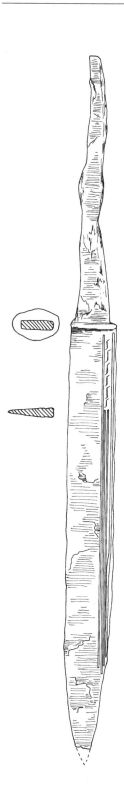

perhaps aided by softwood wedges or glue. It is possible the tang was heated and burned into place, although this would tend to weaken the fabric of the grip. Occasionally knives have metal hilt fittings, either a pommel or both a lower-guard and pommel (**42**). Some authors distinguish between seaxes, having metal fittings, and knives, being without. This seems an arbitrary distinction as there is little reason to suppose that the two forms were functionally different.

While knives are among the most common items found in Anglo-Saxon graves throughout the pagan period, long-seaxes only developed later and are uncommon. Long-seaxes differ little from knives except for their size and the same typology can be applied.

The blade of the seax was sometimes decorated with either incised lines or metal inlays (**colour plate 13**). Decoration is proportionately much more frequent on long-seaxes than knives, the majority of which are plain.

The Sheath

When not in use, knives were kept in a leather sheath. The sheath was often decorated with embossed designs and sometimes trimmed with silver or bronze fittings (**42**). The seax was suspended from the belt with the blade horizontal (**43**), and with the edge uppermost to protect the leather of the sheath. It is unlikely that long-seaxes could be suspended in this manner; given their length it is more likely they were kept in a scabbard similar to that of a sword.

41 *Seax from Northolt Manor, Middlesex, with a long
    tang suitable for use in two hands. Overall length
    60 cm, blade length 36cm.*

(Redrawn by K. R. Dixon after Evison)

Use

The majority of Anglo-Saxons, both men and women, appear to have carried a knife on a daily basis, presumably used for eating and other domestic tasks. While they were not weapons *per se*, warriors presumably took their knives with them when they went to battle, where they might have proved useful for dispatching the seriously wounded. They might also have been used as weapons if domestic disputes led to brawling. In fact, both times the use of a seax is referred to in *Beowulf* it is in circumstances such as these. Firstly, having wrestled Beowulf to the ground, Grendel's mother sits on him, draws her seax and tries to stab him, but the point is unable to penetrate his mail-shirt (line 1545). Secondly, having wounded the dragon, Beowulf draws his *wællseaxe* 'slaughter-seax' to deliver the *coup de grace* (line 2703).

The long-seax developed in the eighth century. Seaxes, presumably long-seaxes, are mentioned in wills alongside other wargear, however, they are rarely mentioned in accounts of battles. It is possible that the long-seax was not primarily a weapon of war, rather that it was designed for hunting. There is some evidence for this since a Frankish pictorial calendar shows two men killing a boar, one of who is using a long-seax.

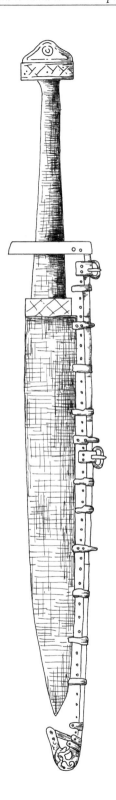

42 *Seax with metal fittings from Ford, Wiltshire. The bronze pommel was silver plated and set with a garnet on one face. The scabbard was trimmed with silver, with silver buckles and a chape with a bird head ornament. Overall length (as drawn) 46cm.*

(Redrawn by K. R. Dixon after Swanton)

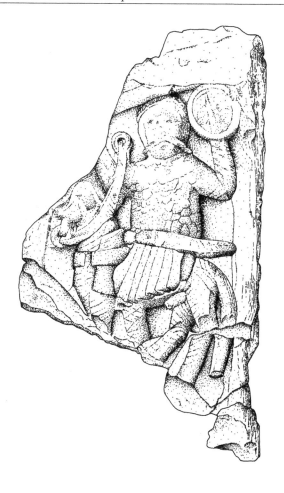

43 *An eighth-century sculpture from Repton, Derbyshire showing a mounted warrior, wearing a mail shirt, with a shield in his left hand and a seax suspended horizontally at his waist. The sculpture was probably part of a funerary monument to a member of the Mercian royal house.*

(Drawn by K. R. Dixon)

The Axe
Æx, Æsc

And sloh hine ða an hiora mid anre æxe yre on ðæt heaford
þæt mid þam dynte he nyþer asah, and his halige blod on þa eorðan feol

One of them struck him with the back of an axe on the head,
so that with the blow he sank down and his holy blood fell on the ground.
(*Anglo-Saxon Chronicle* entry for AD 1012)

The head of the hand axe (**44**) had a very different shape to that of the *francisca*, which is usually assumed to be a missile weapon (see Chapter 2). From the neck, where the head was attached to the haft, the upper and lower edges of the blade narrowed and then curved outward to give a long cutting edge.

At best only fragments of the wooden haft survive, consequently it is difficult to determine the overall size of the axe. The size of the head would suggest it was mounted on a short

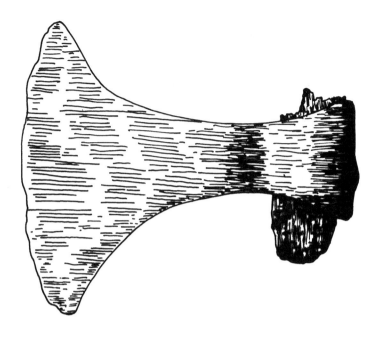

44 *Axehead from Petersfinger, Wiltshire.*
  (Redrawn by K. R. Dixon after Leeds and Shortt)

wooden haft and used one handed, however, the unique all-iron axe-hammer found at Sutton Hoo was mounted on a haft 78cm (31in) long. Axe-hammers were in use on the continent in the sixth century and an example, inlayed with brass and copper, was found at Howletts, Kent, presumably a Merovingian import (**colour plate 12**).

Use

Hand-axes were primarily a tool rather than a weapon. They were rarely deposited in Anglo-Saxon graves or mentioned in heroic literature. They were probably used, much as seaxes were, *in extremis*, by those who had no other weapon.

An axe had several disadvantages compared to a sword. Firstly, because of the relatively short cutting edge it was not possible to cut through both the shield and the opponent with a single blow, a feat that is frequently mentioned in the sagas of sword blows but not of axes. Secondly, because of the triangular cross-section of the blade it would not tend to wound as deeply. Although the axe-head was extremely rugged, the wooden haft could be cut through by an opponent's blows (**45**):

> Then ran up a fellow of Thorir's and smote at Uspak, but he thrust forth his axe, and the blow took the shaft thereof and struck it asunder, and down fell the axe. (*Eyrbyggja Saga*)

73

45 *A detail from the Bayeux tapestry showing an axeman, possibly one of King Harold's brothers, being killed. The head of his axe has been cut from the shaft by his opponents sword cut, a drawback of an axe referred to in Viking sagas.*

(Drawn by K. R. Dixon)

Worse still, the axe shaft could be caught by an opponent and the axe used against its owner:

> Skeggi then seized his axe and struck at Grettir, who on seeing it seized the handle of the axe with his left hand and pulled it forward with such force that Skeggi at once let go. The next moment it stood in his brain and he fell dead to the earth. (*Grettir's Saga*)

1   *Two warriors skirmishing in front of the main line. The archer uses a simple wooden bow with a D-shaped cross-section similar to finds from Nydam, Denmark and wears a bone bracer based on a find from Lowbury, Berkshire. The warrior behind him has a francisca, a small shield and a small seax. (Photograph: K. R. Dixon)*

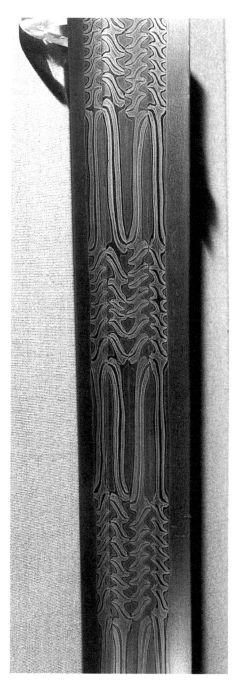 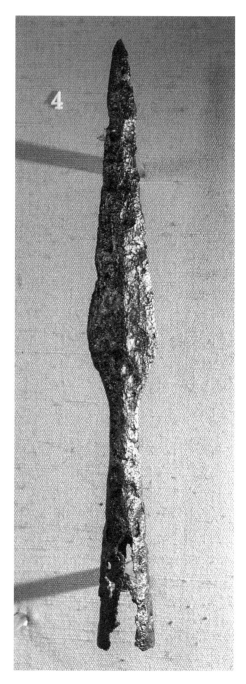

2 Reconstruction of the blade of the sword
   from Sutton Hoo showing the
   distinctive herringbone pattern
   produced by the pattern welding process.
   (Photograph: Author)

3 Spearhead with an angular blade from
   Guildford, Surrey.
   (Photograph: Author)

4 Scene from the eighth-century 'Franks' casket showing an archer defending his hall against a band of warriors. Several of the warriors wear mail shirts. The name Egil appears in runes beneath the scene. Egil was the brother of the mythical Weland Smith and was renowned as an archer, although the tale that the scene depicts is not known. (© The British Museum)

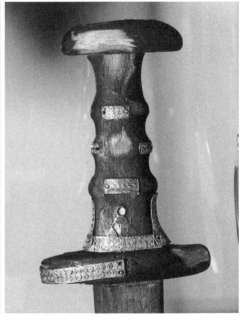

5 Sword hilt and scabbard fittings from Sutton Hoo, Suffolk, with cloisonné decoration of gold and garnet inlay. The two buttons were part of the method of suspension of the scabbard. (© The British Museum)

6 Sword hilt from Cumberland with a grip and guard of horn, decorated with small plates of gold filigree in a spiral pattern and with gold and garnet cloisonné work. The style of the grip suggests an earlier date than the decorative plates which must be at least seventh century. It is quite possible that the decorative plates were a late addition. (Photograph: Author)

7   An eighth-century pommel with filigree decoration from the River Thames near Chiswick, London.
(Photograph courtesy of the Museum of London)

8   Late eighth-century sword hilt from Fetter Lane, London comprising the upper part of the sword grip and the pommel. The hilt was made of silver on an organic base with gilt and niello decoration. The main panels of the grip are decorated on both sides with animal and plant ornament. The facing side has a beast, spread-eagled, on a leafy background, its long tail forming a circular frame to the design. The reverse side has four snakes forming a spiral pattern, again on a background of leaves and stems.
(Photograph: Author)

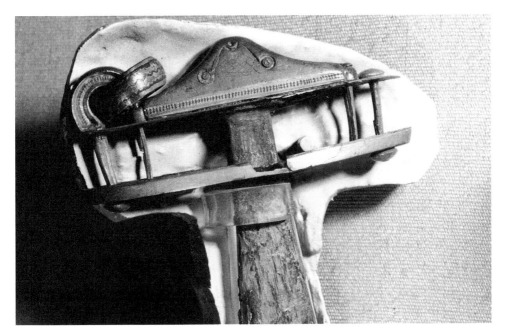

9 Upper part of the hilt of a ring sword from Buckland, Kent. The 'cocked hat' sword pommel
and upper guard are both silver gilt. The two silver rings are decorated
externally with niello zig-zag decoration and on the side have a gilded 'V' shape
depression with ornamental beading. (Photograph: Author)

10 Sword hilt from Crundale Down, Kent, probably late seventh century in date. The
silver gilt pommel is decorated with animal interlace. The two gold mounts for the grip
are decorated with a simple interlace pattern and may have held a foil covering in place.
(Photograph: Author)

11 Early sixth-century decorative scabbard mouth from Chessell Down, Isle of Wight. On the reverse there is a runic inscription ᚫᚳᚩ:ᛋᛟᚱᛁ. This has been transcribed as æco:sœri and translated as 'augmenter of sorrow', which is presumed to be a descriptive name for the sword itself.
(Photograph: Author)

12 A sixth-century axe-hammer from Howletts, Kent. The head is inlayed with brass and copper and was probably a Merovingian import. (Photograph: Author)

13 *Knife blade with the name OSMUND and herringbone decoration inlayed in silver and copper alloy, from the River Thames at Putney, London.*
(Photograph: Author)

14 *Sugar loaf shield boss from East Ewell, Surrey.*
(Photograph: Author)

15 *Two partially gilded copper-alloy shield mounts in the shape of birds of prey from Shelford Farm near Sturry, Kent.*
(Photograph: Author)

16 *Boar crest from the Benty Grange helmet. The boar was associated with the pagan goddess Freyja and symbolised strength.*
(Photograph courtesy of Sheffield City Museum)

*17 Reconstruction of the helmet from Benty Grange, Derbyshire.
(Photograph courtesy of Sheffield City Museum)*

18 *Helmet from the Sutton Hoo ship burial, Suffolk. Only fragments of the original helmet survive, making reconstruction difficult.*
(Photograph: Author)

19 Reconstruction of the helmet from the Sutton Hoo ship burial, Suffolk.
(Photograph: Author)

20 *The eighth-century York helmet.*
   (Photograph courtesy of City of York Council, York Castle Museum)

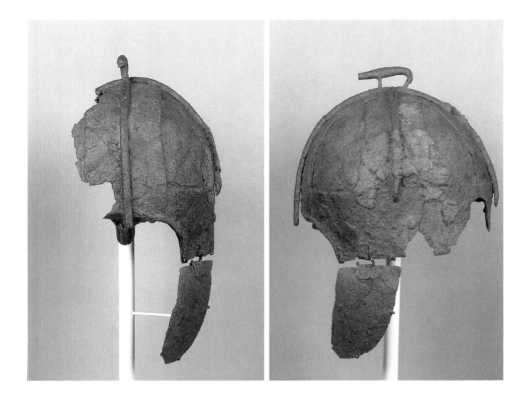

21 The 'Pioneer' helmet from Wallaston, Northamptonshire. The helmet was found with a hanging bowl, a sword and a number of iron belt buckles, on the basis of which it has been dated to the mid seventh century.
(Photograph courtesy Northamptonshire Archaeology)

22 Spangenhelm from Lake Geneva, Switzerland. (Photograph: I Pain)

23 Part of a loose shieldwall fought in open woodland. In this type of fighting a large shield protects the body so that most wounds are to the arms and legs and would not usually be fatal. The warrior must concentrate on several opponents, particularly those on either side of the man he faces as he is more open to a spear thrust from the side than from directly in front. (Photograph: K. R. Dixon)

24 *A heavily armoured theign reviews his troops before a battle. His equipment is of Swedish style. He wears a reconstruction of the seventh century helmet from Ultuna, Sweden, made of interwoven iron bands, a long mail shirt and a pair of iron greaves based on finds from grave 8 at Valsgärde, Sweden. The Valsgärde find has previously been assumed to be body armour but a reconstruction as a set of greaves and a vambrace is more satisfactory. (Photograph: K. R. Dixon)*

25 *A heavily armoured warrior confronts a skirmisher. Despite their proximity neither poses
any great threat to the other; the swordsman is well protected from the skirmisher's javelin
by his large shield, helmet and mail while the lightly armed skirmisher could
easily outrun his opponent if he attempted to close to within swords reach. The armoured
warriors helmet is a reconstruction of the spangenhelm from Batajnica, Yugoslavia and is
fitted with a horse-hair plume. (Photograph: K. R. Dixon)*

4 Protective equipment

Hwanon ferigeað ge fætte scyldas
græge syrcan ond grimhelmas

From where do you bring these broad shields,
grey mail-shirts and fierce helmets?
(*Beowulf,* 333)

After the spear, the shield was the most common item of wargear for the Anglo-Saxon warrior. Nearly a quarter of male burials contain evidence of a shield. In contrast, the other types of protective equipment, helmets and ring-mail body armour, were reserved for only the richest and most important. Only four helmets have been found, all bar one elaborately decorated. Mail, although frequently described in verse, has only survived once, in the richest Anglo-Saxon burial ever found, Sutton Hoo.

The Shield
Scyld, Lind (Lime-wood), Rond (Round), Bord (Board)

fugelas singað
gylleð græhama guðwudu hlynneð
scyld scefte oncwyð

... ravens sing,
the grey wolf yells, war-wood sounds,
shield answers shaft.
(*Finnsburh,* 5)

Anglo-Saxon shields were made from a circular wooden board, at the centre of which was fitted an iron 'boss' (**46**). The board behind the boss was cut away and a grip fitted across the opening, by which the shield was held. The shield was often covered with leather and decorated with fittings of iron or bronze.

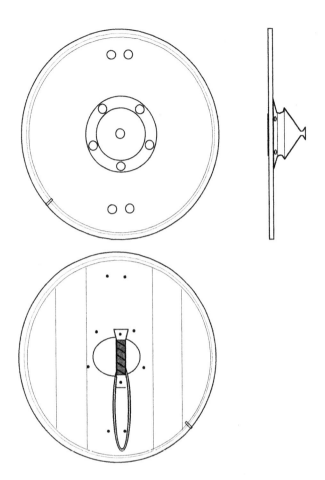

46   *Reconstruction of a 'typical' Anglo-Saxon shield. The shield consisted of a board made up of planks, covered and rimmed with leather. In the centre was an iron boss attached to the board by five iron rivets. The board behind the boss was cut away and a grip fitted across the opening, by which the shield was held. The shield was decorated with two pairs of iron rivets.*

(Redrawn by R. Underwood after Dickinson & Härke)

The Board

Although in Anglo-Saxon poetry shields are only ever referred to as being made of lime, a variety of species were in fact used, and lime or linden-wood was rare. The most common are alder, willow and poplar, although maple, birch, ash and oak were also used. Alder, willow and poplar are particularly suitable for this purpose, being tough yet comparatively light.

The size of Anglo-Saxon shields recovered from burials is inferred from impressions in the soil, the position of remaining fittings and the dimensions of the grave. The evidence suggests that boards varied significantly in size, between 0.34 and 0.92m (1-3ft) in diameter, with the majority in the range 0.46 to 0.66m (1 ½ to 2¼ feet). The largest shields are all late in date, which may indicate a gradual change in the nature of conflict.

In comparison to the continent, where quite a number of complete shield boards have survived, Anglo-Saxon shields appear small. Continental finds are typically 80-100cm (2ft 8in-3ft 4in) diameter, although smaller shields have been found. This may not represent a real divergence in tradition, however, rather the sample of shields from graves for which the size can be estimated may be biased; a large shield might have been more likely to have been placed upright against the side of the grave, rather than horizontal on the floor, which would mean that when it was excavated its size would not be able to be estimated. Alternatively, it may simply reflect the selection of smaller shields for inclusion in the English burial rite.

The thickness of the shield board also varied, between 5mm and 13mm (1/5 in-½in) although the majority of boards were in the range 6-8mm (¼in-1/5in). From the dimensions of the board the weight of the shield can be estimated to have varied from less than 3kg (about 6lbs) to around 5kg (11lbs).

The board was made up of planks of solid wood; early identifications of 'plywood' shields appear to have been erroneous. The number of planks would clearly depend on the size of the shield and probably ranged from as few as three up to nine or more. The method by which the planks were held together is not known, but it is likely they were glued.

The board was often covered with leather on either the front only or on both front and back. The leather would serve to strengthen the board and to hold the planks together. Archaeological evidence for covers of cow hide is corroborated by the Laws of Æthelstan (AD 926-930) which stipulate that sheepskin should not be used in the making of shields. The rim may have been separately bound with leather; pictorial representations of shields sometimes show a 'raised rim' suggesting a leather edging (**47**).

Although all the complete shields found in continental deposits have flat boards, pictorial and poetic evidence suggest some shields were convex. Convex boards could be made by bending planks after softening them in steam or boiling oil, or by shaping the board from thicker planks.

Anglo-Saxon shields may have been painted, although physical evidence is lacking; 'bright' and 'yellow' shields are referred to in *Beowulf*. Finds of Danish shields from this period show traces of red paint, while the Viking shields from the Gokstad ship were painted black and yellow. Alternatively, the leather covering of the shield might itself have been dyed or chosen for its colour.

Depictions of shields in continental and Viking art frequently show the shield board decorated with a pattern of curved lines emanating from the boss. This may not be a purely decorative feature; a ninth-century Frankish illustration shows these curved lines accompanied by what appears to be lines of stitches, giving the appearance of a leather cover made in panels (**48**). The curving pattern would have been a natural way to cover a convex shield without requiring undue stretching of the leather.

a

b

47   *Helmet plates from Vendel, Sweden:*

a   *Two warriors engaged in single combat. One of the warriors carries a shield decorated with studs which has been pierced by his opponent's spear.*

b   *Two heavily armoured warriors. Each warrior's scabbard is suspended from a baldric by a pair of buttons and one of the warriors has a ring-sword. Their spears are bound with piece of fabric, possibly marking the balance point.*

(Drawn by K. R. Dixon)

48   *A detail from the ninth-century Stuttgart Psalter showing a shield with a stitched leather covering.*

(Drawn by K. R. Dixon)

The Boss

An iron boss, mounted at the centre of the board, covered the grip and protected the knuckles (**49**). The forms of boss can be divided into two main groups, based on their method of manufacture.

The most common form, 'carinated', developed from the continental tradition during the fifth century and continued in use until at least the middle of the seventh century and possibly later. The form developed over time (**50**). The apex of the boss was often formed into a 'button', up to 6cm in diameter. The button was sometimes decorated with silver or gold plating or capped with an elaborate bronze mount. The method of manufacture of the carinated boss is unclear, but it is likely that they were either formed from a single billet of iron or that the cone was made from a billet with the wall and flange being made from a separate iron sheet and the two parts welded together around the rim (**51**). The button was either formed with the boss or inserted later and welded into place.

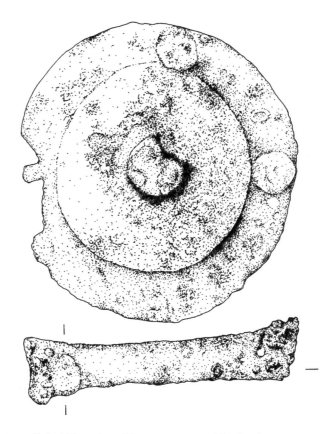

49   *A 'carinated' shield boss from Norton cemetery, Cleveland.*

(Redrawn by K. R. Dixon after Sherlock & Welch)

In contrast 'tall cone' bosses (**53**) were made from a sheet or sheets of iron with welds running from the rim to the apex (**52**). They range from very simple straight sided cones formed from a single sheet to curved 'sugar loaf' forms which retain the wall and button of earlier styles but reach up to 200mm (8in) in height (**colour plate 14**). Both forms of tall cone bosses became popular in the seventh century but continued in use until much later.

The boss was attached to the board with iron, or occasionally bronze, rivets. Usually four or five rivets were used, equally spaced around the rim, although bosses have been found with up to twelve rivets. The heads were generally broad, 15-20mm (3/5in- 4/5in) in diameter, and sometimes silvered or tinned. The lower end of the rivet was usually hammered flat, sometimes over an iron or bronze washer, or simply bent over at right angles.

Traces of organic material found inside the boss suggest that the interior may have been padded to prevent injury to the hand.

50   *The form of the carinated boss developed over time, although there was probably considerable overlap between styles:*

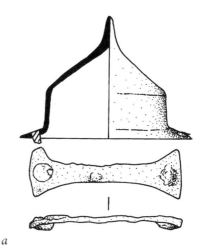

a

a   *Tall cone with a pointed apex, c. AD 475.*

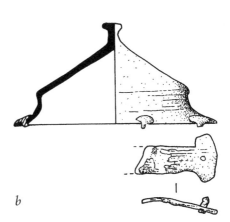

b

b   *Low cone with the apex formed into a button, c. AD 525.*

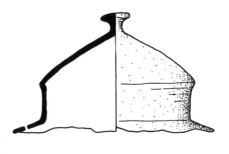

c

c   *Rounded cone with button, AD 575.*

(Redrawn by K. R. Dixon after Dickinson & Härke)

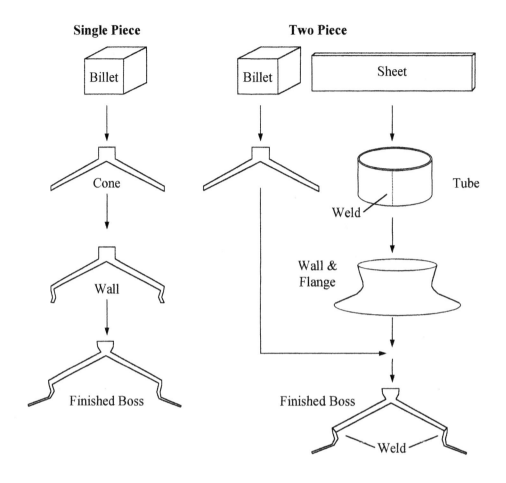

Single Piece

Billet

Cone

Wall

Finished Boss

Two Piece

Billet

Sheet

Weld

Tube

Wall &
Flange

Finished Boss

Weld

51   *Possible methods of construction of carinated shield bosses.*

(Redrawn by R. Underwood after Salter)

The Grip

The shield was held by an iron grip that spanned the hole in the board behind the boss. The majority of grips were nothing more than a short strap 10-16cm (4-6in) long , the sides either straight or gently curved to fit the hand (**54**). A few short grips had flanges which would have enclosed a wooden handle. The grip was riveted to the board at either end. A minority of shields were furnished with much longer grips. The middle portion of these grips, was almost always flanged and was riveted to the board in the usual way but narrow strips extended on either side of the grip. The terminals of these strips could be circular, club shaped or bifurcated, and were again riveted to the board.

52   *A 'tall straight cone' boss from Portsdown, Hants, showing the seam that demonstrates the method of manufacture.*

(Drawn by K. R. Dixon)

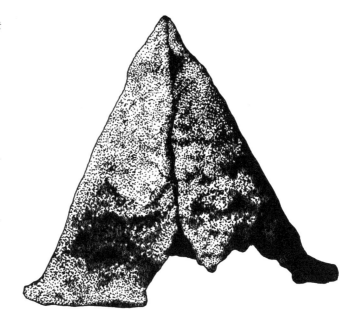

53   *Tall cone bosses: a Tall straight cone without carination, c.AD 650;*

b   *Tall straight cone with carination, c. AD 650;*

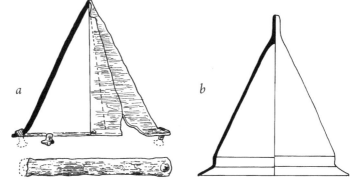

c   *Sugar loaf, c. AD 675.*

(Redrawn by K.R. Dixon after Evison)

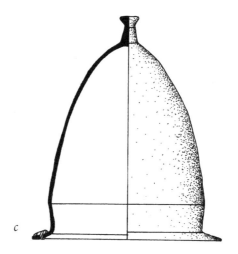

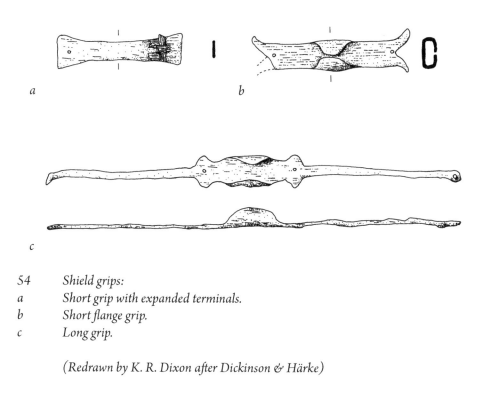

a

b

c

54   Shield grips:
a   *Short grip with expanded terminals.*
b   *Short flange grip.*
c   *Long grip.*

(*Redrawn by K. R. Dixon after Dickinson & Härke*)

The thin iron grip was built up to the shape of the hand using either a cloth or leather binding or a wooden handle, which could itself be wrapped in cloth or leather (**55**). The handle could be made in one piece with the board or made from a separate piece of wood.

Decorative Fittings

The majority of shields show no evidence of decoration, however, just under half of the shields found have metal fittings which have no discernible purpose and were therefore presumably decorative.

By far the most common decorative feature was studs or discs of iron or, occasionally, tinned bronze (**56**). These were usually arranged in two pairs on either side of the boss. An alternative, asymmetrical, arrangement of studs is shown on two of the plates attached to a seventh-century helmet from Vendel, Sweden (**47**). A few shields were decorated with silvered or gilt bronze appliqués. These were either zoomorphic or geometric. Zoomorphic forms include fish, birds and quadrupeds. They are usually found in opposing pairs arranged on either side of the boss. Less elaborate iron lozenge shaped fittings may have been decorative or may have been fitted as repairs to the board.

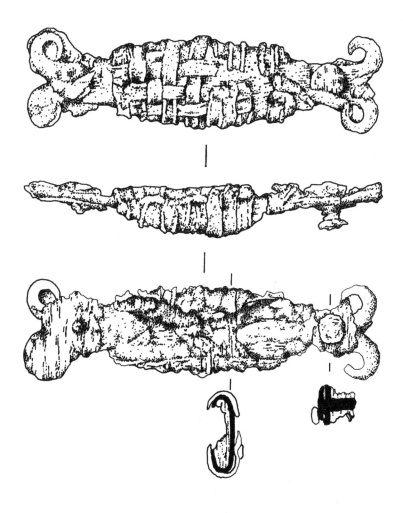

55   *An iron grip enclosing a wooden handle and bound with woven leather strips, from Morning Thorpe cemetery, Norfolk. Traces of textile were also found which may have served as additional padding.*

   (Redrawn by K. R. Dixon after Green et al.)

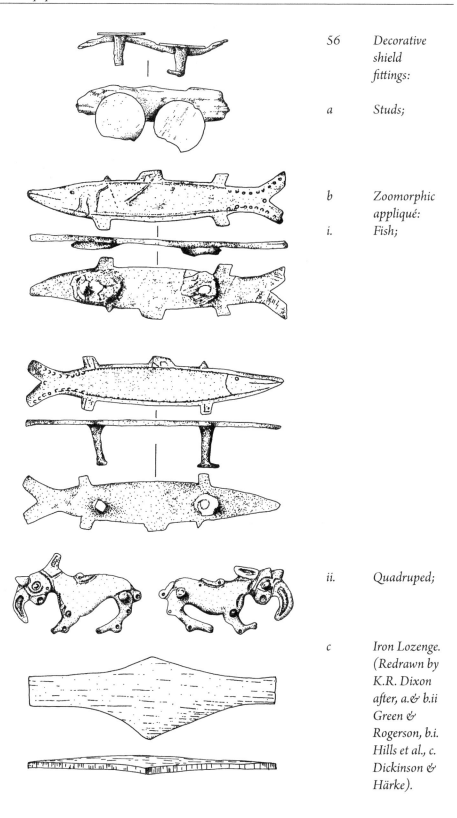

56   *Decorative shield fittings:*

a   *Studs;*

b   *Zoomorphic appliqué:*
i.   *Fish;*

ii.   *Quadruped;*

c   *Iron Lozenge. (Redrawn by K.R. Dixon after, a.& b.ii Green & Rogerson, b.i. Hills et al., c. Dickinson & Härke).*

Short iron and bronze U-sectioned strips are occasionally found and may be the remains of edge bindings from shields. These could have protected a vulnerable portion of the edge of the shield from wear or may have covered the join in the leather rim. The exceptional shield from Sutton Hoo, Suffolk, has a complete bronze rim which was both sewn onto the board and clipped at intervals with bronze strips riveted in place.

Some shields may have been fitted with leather straps to allow the shield to be slung on the back when not in use. It is possible that the decorative studs served to attach the strap to the back of the board, although many of the studs appear unsuitable for this purpose. Alternatively a simple strap of leather tied to the grip may have sufficed.

Use

The shield was the only piece of defensive equipment available to most Anglo-Saxon warriors, and few, if any, would have gone to battle without one. Perhaps more than the spear, which had a dual use as a tool for hunting, it distinguished a man as a warrior. Tacitus noted that the supreme disgrace for a Germanic warrior was to lose his shield in battle.

The apparent variation in the size of shields should not, perhaps, be surprising and may reflect variations in the style of warfare.

A small shield is by virtue of its size much lighter and more manoeuvrable. It is therefore more suited to single combat or small skirmishes. Its manoeuvrability means that the more durable boss can usually be used to parry the blow, rather than the wooden board. Also, it can be used to deflect blows in a more controlled manner and the complex shape of the boss, both the carination and the button apex, assist in this by tending to 'capture' the opponent's sword. *In extremis* the shield can even be used as a weapon, using either the rim or the spiked boss. Small shields also have the mundane advantage that, in a society where violence is, to a greater or lesser extent, endemic, a small shield can be more easily carried around on a daily basis.

In contrast larger shields are more useful in pitched battles, particularly against missile weapons. In single combat, while the large board gives greater protection this is balanced by the fact that it is less manoeuvrable and the size of the board tends to screen from view the movements of the enemy. In the shieldwall, however, larger shields are essential as each man is vulnerable not only to the man facing him but to those men one or even two positions removed in the line. The warrior therefore relies on the passive protection of his own, and his comrades, shields (**57**). Similarly, while it is possible to parry a single arrow with a small shield by concentrating on the archer, in the confusion of a large battle missiles would have tended to appear from nowhere; consequently the only defence was the protection afforded by a shield covering the greater part of the body.

Literary sources suggest that shields would often be damaged in battle; there are frequent references in poetry to shields splitting under repeated sword blows and

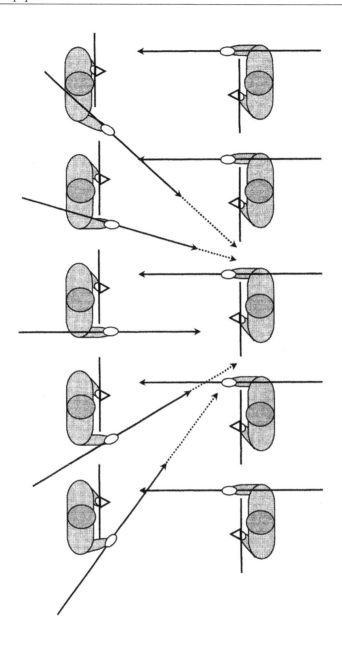

57   *In a shieldwall a warrior could be attacked by at least five of the enemy front rank. He would have relied on the protection of his shield and those of his comrades. It would have been essential to maintain the integrity of the line, neither stepping too far forward nor being forced back, or some of the warriors would have become exposed to enemy attacks. It is unlikely that shields were overlapped once the opposing shieldwalls closed to within striking range as this reduces the mobility of the shield and prevents it being moved to parry enemy blows.*
     (Drawn by R. Underwood)

spears, thrown or thrust, could pierce the board as shown on one of the helmet plates from Vendel, Sweden (**47**). Experienced warriors could try to reduce the damage by tilting the shield to deflect the blow or by receiving the blow on the iron boss. While more difficult to make, curved shields have advantages over simple flat shields. In particular, the curved surface tends to deflect all but the most direct blows reducing damage to the board.

Damaged shields were often repaired, or if the damage was too great the iron fittings could be reused on a new board. Several bosses have been found with a second set of empty rivet holes in the flange indicating reuse. Even though the majority of the damage would have been to the wooden board, nearly a third of surviving bosses show evidence of some damage prior to being buried. The iron boss could be repaired with patches of iron or bronze welded or riveted over the damaged area, usually from the inside of the boss, indicating that the shield had been disassembled prior to the repair.

Literary evidence also suggests that shields, presumably by the nature of their decoration, helped to identify individuals. On three separate occasions the author of the poem *The Battle of Maldon* refers to warriors lifting their shield aloft before making a speech. Presumably such an action, if it is more than just a literary device, would alert the surrounding warriors to where their leader was and that he was still alive, even if they could not hear the words he spoke.

Mail
Byrne, Heresyrce (Battle-shirt), Herenet (Battle-net), Hringnet (Ring-net),

Da gewat him wund hæleð on wæg gangan
sæde þæt his byrne abrocen wære
heresceorp unhror and eac wæs his helm ðyrel

Then a wounded man went on his way,
said that his byrnie was broken,
his armour useless and also was his helmet pierced.
(*Finnsburh*, 43)

Although referred to frequently in literature, mail is found very rarely in Anglo-Saxon burials. The absence of finds is not entirely surprising however, as mail survives only rarely from antiquity, even from periods when it is known to have been widely available. The only complete Anglo-Saxon mail shirt found to date comes from Sutton Hoo, Suffolk. The mail is badly corroded, which prevents detailed examination. The rings are 8mm (1/3 in) in diameter and some were closed with copper rivets, indicating that the mail was probably made of alternate rows of riveted and forged or welded rings. The shirt is believed to have been at least hip length and the extant remains weigh 11kg (25lb). A similar shirt was found at Vimose, Denmark, dating to the fourth or fifth century (**58**). The long shirt with short sleeves consists of about 20,000 riveted iron rings.

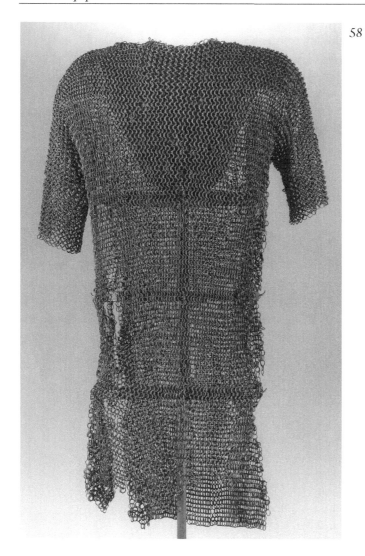

58   *Mail shirt from Vimose, Denmark, comprising over 20,000 links.*

(Photograph courtesy of the National Museum, Copenhagen)

Mail was also found in association with the York helmet and it has been fully conserved, allowing the method of construction to be determined. The surviving mail is 105mm (4in) from top to bottom and, when fully extended, 470mm (19in) at its widest. It consists of nearly 2000 links arranged in horizontal rows, formed alternately of welded and lapped and riveted rings. The rings have an external diameter of 8mm (1/25in) and are made of circular cross section wire of 1mm (1/3in) diameter. The mail is made with each ring passing through two rings in the row above and two in the row below. Adjacent rings within a row are not linked, but pass through the same ring in both the row above and below. This appears to have been the standard method of making mail. Fragments of a mail shirt from Thorsbjerg, Denmark show the same alternating rows of welded and riveted rings (**59**).

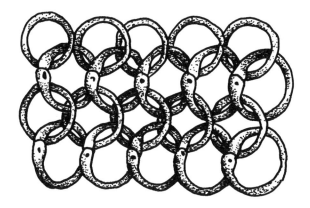

59　　*Section of the mail shirt from the Thorsbjerg bog deposit. It is made up of links arranged in horizontal rows, formed alternately of welded and riveted rings.*

(*Redrawn by K. R. Dixon after Engelhardt*)

The rings of the York mail were made from drawn wire. Drawing is a technique whereby wire is made by pulling an iron rod through a series of successively smaller holes. The rings would then have been formed by winding the wire around a rod to form a coil, and cutting the coil along its length. The rings were made larger than the size required and then reduced in diameter leaving an overlap. Half the rings were then welded closed by heating to white heat and striking sharply with a hammer. The remaining rings were prepared for riveting by flattening the overlapping ends and drilling a hole for the rivet. The open and welded rings were then linked together and the prepared rings closed with an iron rivet.

Mail is worn by several figures on the eighth-century Franks casket (**colour plate 4**). They appear to wear hip length shirts, with long sleeves, not dissimilar to that found at Vimose.

Use

Mail would provide a significant degree of protection against most of the weapons used in the Anglo-Saxon period. While no armour could mitigate all the effects of a well placed blow delivered with force, mail could convert a potentially fatal blow into a wound, while a weak or glancing blow might do little injury. This would have given a very significant advantage to an armoured warrior, given the danger of a man receiving a retaliatory blow if he failed to kill or seriously injure an opponent having closed to within striking range.

Mail is most effective against cutting blows, for example from a sword, where the weight of the blow is distributed across many mail links. Thrusts, for example from a spear, concentrate the force of the blow on only a few links; a strong blow will therefore tend to burst open the links and penetrate the mail, often driving links into the body.

Mail would rust quickly if not properly cared for. Ancient authors recognised this; the handbook of military strategy (*Strategikon*) attributed to the Byzantine Emperor Maurice (AD 582-602) mentions the use of leather cases to protect mail byrnies from the elements when not in use. If rust were allowed to form it would have to be removed, probably by shaking the mail with sand. While this is a relatively simple process, it would, over time, abrade and weaken the links and must therefore have only been performed infrequently.

Mail armour had one main disadvantage, its weight. The majority of the weight is borne on the shoulders, although this can be mitigated by wearing a waist-belt over the mail which transfers some of the load to the hips. A fit man would have little difficulty if the fighting was largely static, but would be severely disadvantaged in skirmish actions or if the battle lines moved quickly, particularly if the battlefield sloped adversely.

The Helmet
Helm

ac se hwita helm   hafelan werede
...   since geweorðad
befongen freawrasnum   swa hine fyrndagum
worhte wæpna smið   wundrum teode
besette swinlicum   þæt hine syðþan no
brond ne beadomecas   bitan ne meahton

And the bright helmet   the head guarded,
... artfully crafted,
encircled with fine mail,   as it in days of old
the weapon smith had wrought,   wonderfully adorned,
set with boar images,   that it afterwards no
sword nor battle-blade   might bite.
(*Beowulf*, 1448)

To date only four Anglo-Saxon helmets have been found, although fragments of several other possible helmets have been identified. All four helmets show significant differences in their construction and ornamentation.

The Sutton Hoo Helmet

The earliest dated helmet is from the Sutton Hoo ship burial in Suffolk (**colour plates 18 and 19**). It is believed that the grave belonged to the East Anglian king Rædwald, who died in AD 624/5 although the helmet may have been old when it was buried

60   *Detail of a figure of a warrior from one of the four dies for stamping helmet plates from Torslunda, Sweden. The warrior has a boar crest on his helmet and a ring mounted on his sword hilt.*

(Drawn by K. R. Dixon)

and may date from as early as the first quarter of the sixth century. Only fragments of the helmet survive but it is believed to have originally weighed approximately 2.5kg (5 ½ lb).

The bowl of the Sutton Hoo helmet is made from a single piece of metal to which were attached cheek-pieces, a rigid metal neck guard and a face-mask. The bowl is reinforced with a hollow iron half-round crest in the shape of a 'dragon', inlaid with silver wire and with a head at both front and back. The gilded heads are beautifully formed with open mouths showing rows of teeth, garnet eyes and punched work decoration.

The features on the face-mask and the front of the helmet, eyebrows, nose and moustache, are grouped to form a second 'dragon'. This dragon faces upwards, nose to nose with the head of the dragon crest. Its extended wings are the eyebrows above the eyeholes in the face-mask, elaborately decorated with niello striations above a band of garnet cloisonné. The tips of the wings themselves terminate in much smaller gilded animal heads. The nose and moustache form the body and tail of the dragon, gilded and decorated with incised lines. Finally, a simple gilded segment of a circle protrudes from below the tail suggesting the mouth.

The face-mask, cheek-pieces, neck guard and the majority of the bowl were elaborately decorated with embossed foil plates of tinned bronze (*Pressblech*). Five designs can be identified. Each occurs several times indicating they were stamped with a set of dies, similar to the dies found at Torslunda, Sweden (**60**). Two of the designs are of zoomorphic interlace. Of the remaining three, only two can be reconstructed. One

a

b

61   *Helmet plates from the Sutton Hoo ship burial.*
a   *A mounted warrior, with a spear and shield, rides down a mailed warrior. In turn the
      mailed warrior is stabbing the mounted warriors horse. A diminutive third figure
      crouches by the cavalryman's shoulder and guides his spear.*
b   *Two warriors, each wearing an elaborate 'horned' helmet and holding a sword and
      two spears engaged in a ritual dance. The second-century writer Tacitus described
      young men of Germanic tribes performing such a ritual dance with spears and swords.
      (Redrawn by K. R. Dixon after Bruce Mitford)*

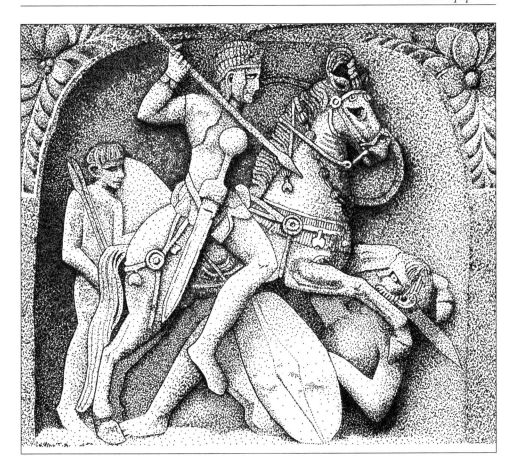

62   *The first-century tombstone of Titus Flavius Bassus a trooper in the Roman cavalry, now in the Römisch-Germanisches Museum, Cologne, Germany. The composition of the scene has close parallels to the 'rider' scene on the Sutton Hoo helmet. The elite cavalry units, the alae, were recruited almost exclusively from barbarian tribes including the Germans. This type of tombstone has no Roman or Italian prototype and is mainly found in the Rhineland and Britain.*

(Drawn by K. R. Dixon).

shows a mounted warrior, with a spear and shield, riding down a mailed warrior who in turn is stabbing the mounted warrior's horse (**61**). A diminutive third figure crouches by the cavalryman's shoulder and guides his spear. The second plate shows two warriors, each wearing an elaborate 'horned' helmet and holding a sword and two spears apparently engaged in a ritual dance. Only fragments of the third design survive and its position cannot be identified. It is possible it was part of a repair made before the helmet was buried.

The face-mask was covered with a single sheet of foil stamped repeatedly with one of the two interlace patterns. The remainder of the helmet was covered with individual plates stamped with a single design. The plates were attached to the helmet with fluted strips of bronze foil which were riveted in place.

The style of decoration, and in particular the composition of the decorative plates, show remarkable similarities with helmets found in Sweden at Vendel and Valsgärde and with dies used to make similar plates from Torslunda. It has therefore been suggested that the Sutton Hoo helmet was either made in England by a Swedish craftsman or was imported from Sweden. However, the composition of both of the surviving scenes was extremely traditional and there are close parallels in England and Germany as well as in Scandinavia. The 'rider' scene also has parallels in first-century Roman cavalry tombstones (**62**).

Both scenes probably had religious associations. The dancing warriors have horned helmets and appear to be engaged in a ritual dance. On the Valsgärde helmet there is a close parallel to the Sutton Hoo 'rider' scene, however, the diminutive figure guiding the rider's spear also has horns. The association of horned figures and religious rites dates back to the Bronze Age. By the Anglo-Saxon period horned figures were probably associated with the god Woden and might be thought to bring good luck, particularly in battle. Tacitus, writing in the second century, describes a ritual dance among the Germanic tribes, apparently similar to that depicted on the Sutton Hoo helmet:

> They have only one kind of public show, which is performed without variation at every festive gathering. Naked youths, trained to the sport, dance about among swords and spears levelled at them. Practice begets skill, and skill grace; but they are not professionals and do not receive payment. Their most daring flings have their only reward in the pleasure they give the spectators.

The construction of the Sutton Hoo helmet and the use of metal foil decoration appears to derive from late Roman 'ridged' helmets of the fourth and fifth century (**63**). The ridged helmet found at Burgh Castle (**64**) may have belonged to a Germanic warrior serving in the Roman Army since two franciscas (see Chapter 2), traditionally Germanic weapons, were also found.

A possible fragment of a helmet crest similar to that from Sutton Hoo was found at Rempstone, Nottinghamshire and another at Icklingham, Suffolk. Also a fragment of silver *Pressblech* foil, bearing the head, shoulder and right hand of another dancing warrior, similar to the Sutton Hoo helmet decorative plates, was found in a robbed seventh-century tumulus in Caenby, Lincolnshire (**65**). Although these finds cannot be conclusively shown to come from helmets, they do suggest that helmets were rather more common than might otherwise be thought.

63   *Late Roman 'Ridge helmet' from Berkasova, Yugoslavia. Helmets such as this may have been the inspiration for the Sutton Hoo helmet.*

(Photograph courtesy of the Vojvodjanski Museum, Novi Sad)

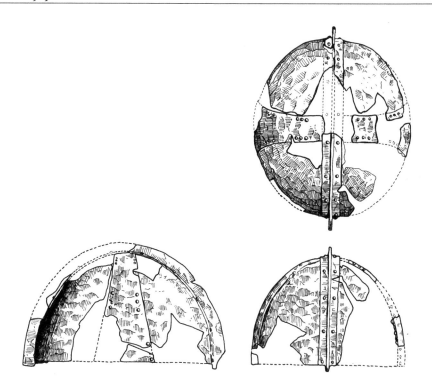

64   *Late Roman 'Ridge helmet' from Burgh Castle. The helmet may have belonged to a*
        Germanic warrior serving in the Roman Army.

        (Redrawn by K. R. Dixon after Johnson).

The Benty Grange Helmet

The helmet found at Benty Grange in Derbyshire (**colour plate 17**) has been dated to the mid seventh century. It is constructed from seven iron bands, with the shape defined by the brow band, the crest band and a lateral band. The crest and lateral band both extend below the brow band to form a nasal guard and a neck guard. Four additional short bands run from the brow band to the lateral band. The gaps between the bands were filled with plates of moulded horn and traces of horn below the rivet heads suggest the bands themselves were also covered with horn, presumably as decoration.

The crest is surmounted by a figure of a boar (**colour plate 16**). The boar is made of two D-section bronze tubes riveted together, leaving a gap running from the head to the tail. In the reconstruction this gap is filled with a plume of horsehair. The boar stands on two iron legs and is riveted to the crest band. The features are carefully picked out; it has garnet eyes, in beaded gold mounts, and gilded inlayed tusks and ears, while the body of the boar is decorated with silver-gilt studs and larger plates marking the shoulders and hips.

65 *Fragment of foil showing a
    'horned' warrior, possibly from
    a helmet plate, from Caenby,
    Lincolnshire.*

    *(Redrawn by K. R. Dixon
    after Bruce Mitford)*

In contrast the nasal guard is decorated with a silver cross. The arms of the cross are slightly flared and emanate from a central roundel. The four arms were made equal but the lower arm was lengthened with a extra strip of silver. The cross is flanked by two zigzag lines of silver studs.

The only other decorative feature are the heads of the rivets on the iron bands which are formed into 'double axe heads' of silver.

Boar images are commonly associated with helmets. The boar was associated with the pagan goddess Freyja and symbolised strength. This association was long standing; Tacitus, wrote of the Baltic Aesttii:

> They worship the mother of the gods, and wear as emblems of this cult the masks of boars, which stand them in stead of armour or human protection and ensure the safety of the worshipper even among his enemies.

Boar crests are depicted on one of the dies from Torslunda, Sweden, (**60**) and described in Beowulf:

> *þonne heoru bunden,   hamere geþuren,*
> *sweord swate fah   swin ofer helme*
> *ecgum dyhttig   andweard sireð.*

> … when the blade bound,   hammer forged,
> sword blood stained,   the boar over helmets,
> mighty of edge,   shears through.
> (*Beowulf*, 1285)

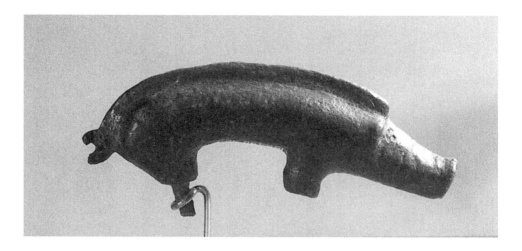

66   *Boar figure, probably the crest of a helmet, from Guilden Morden, Cambridgeshire.
(Photograph: Author)*

A bronze boar, very similar to the Benty Grange crest, was found in a grave at Guilden Morden, Cambridgeshire. The grave was probably a woman's which suggests that the crest was detached from the helmet in antiquity.

The contradiction of the use of the pagan boar image and the overtly Christian cross has led to the suggestion that the helmet was in use for some time before the cross decoration was added. While this cannot be disproved it should be noted that the Beowulf poet, although a Christian, had no qualms about describing pagan boar images and that the York helmet also uses boar images, albeit less overtly, alongside Christian inscriptions.

The York Helmet

The helmet from Coppergate, York (**colour plate 20**) has been dated to the mid to late eighth century and is thus Anglian rather than Viking. It comprises a bowl made of iron plates, hinged iron cheek-pieces and a mail curtain protecting the back of the neck. Like the Benty Grange helmet the iron bowl is made up from a brow band, a crest band and a lateral band although these are much broader; as a consequence there are no interstitial bands. Instead, the gaps between the bands are filled with beaten iron plates. The brow-band is cut away to form deep eyeholes and the crest band extends to form a nasal guard which is strengthened and decorated with a cast bronze plate. This nasal plate is decorated with an animal interlace design and extends as 'eyebrows' over the arched eyeholes. The eyebrows are decorated with incised lines and terminate in small canine heads. All the edges of the bowl and cheek plates are bound with bronze. At the rear of the bowl the mail curtain is suspended from the binding, which has a series of slots cut into it and a wire running inside of it. Bronze rings pass through the slots and are threaded over the wire. The mail curtain then hangs from these bronze rings.

The bowl has a low bronze crest running from front to back with a second subsidiary crest running from side to side. The crest is formed from five separate pieces; the flat inscribed strip is flanked by two rods decorated with twisting incised lines and edged with two bronze strips formed into hollow D-sectioned tubes. At the front, the crest terminates in a cast animal head with incised features. At the sides and rear the twisting rods of the crest come together as opposing animal heads.

The two crests both bear the same inscription:

INNOMINE·DNI·NOSTRI·IHV·SCS·SPS·DI·ET·
OMNIBVS·DECEMVS·AMEN·OSHERE·XPI

'In the name of our Lord Jesus Christ, the Holy Spirit (and) God; and
to all we say Amen, Oshere'

Oshere is an Anglo-Saxon name, most probably the owner of the helmet.

The cheek-plates are undecorated except for the bronze binding strip. They are attached to the helmet bowl with an iron hinge. In the middle of each cheek piece is evidence of a rivet by which a chin strap would have been attached. Four bronze hooks are attached to the back edges of the cheek-plates and hold the mail curtain in place.

The helmet shows some evidence of use in battle. A V-shaped dent on the left-hand front infill plate has been interpreted as being from an arrow or possibly a thrown spear and a nick in the nasal may be the result of a glancing blow with a sword. Obviously the damage may have had a more mundane cause.

The Pioneer Helmet

The 'Pioneer' helmet was discovered in March 1997 in a large gravel quarry at Wollaston, near Wellingborough in Northamptonshire. It was found together with a hanging bowl, a sword with a grip without metal fitments and a number of iron belt buckles, on the basis of which it has been dated to the mid seventh century. It consists of a plain iron cap similar in construction to the York helmet but with little evidence of decoration except for a boar crest (**colour plate 21**).

The cap is formed of a brow band, a crest band and a lateral band with the gaps between filled with beaten iron plates, the whole held together by iron rivets. The cap is undecorated except for three shallow parallel incised lines, which run down the edges of the bands and may have served to partially conceal the rivet heads. The brow band is cut away to form deep eyeholes and the crest band extends to form a nasal guard. The eyeholes are edged with strips of iron which extend part-way down the nasal guard and the edge of the nasal guard is burred over to form a raised edge. The nasal guard appears to have been bent inward prior to being buried, making the helmet unwearable. Both the crest and lateral bands are reinforced with simple D-section iron ribs, which were riveted to the cap. The bowl is surmounted by a boar crest, however, this is simply formed of iron and much less elaborate that on the Benty Grange helmet.

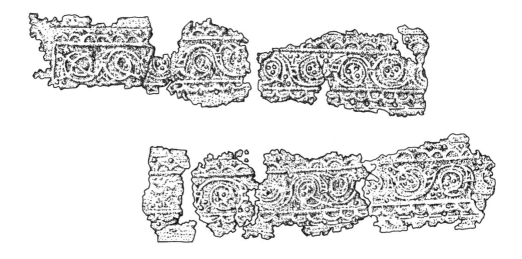

67   *Fragments of foil, possibly the browband of a Spangenhelm, from Dumfriesshire.*

(Redrawn by K. R. Dixon after De Paor)

The helmet is fitted with cheek pieces, which are attached to the helmet with simple wire loops. In the middle of each cheek piece is a rivet by which a chinstrap would have been attached.

X-rays of the helmet taken shortly after its discovery appeared to show evidence of a neck guard composed of strips of iron, however, no material could be recovered during conservation. It is now believed that these were the remains of belt fittings and not associated with the helmet.

A gingery brown deposit, which could be the remains of a leather lining, was preserved in the corrosion of the interior of the bowl. This is the first evidence of a helmet lining, although it is likely that all Anglo-Saxon helmets had a padded lining of some form to absorb the force of a blow.

Spangenhelms

The most common form of helmet in use on the continent in the sixth and seventh century was the spangenhelm (**colour plate 22**). Over two dozen have been found, mainly in France, Germany, Italy and the Balkans. While there is no conclusive evidence for the use of spangenhelms in Britain, fragments of gold foil from Dumfriesshire may be part of the browband of a spangenhelm (**67**).

The spangenhelms found in western Europe are remarkably uniform and their production is believed to have centred around Ostrogothic Italy. They were made of between four and six iron plates shaped into a bowl and held together by bronze bands (*Spangen*) which were riveted to the plates. The *Spangen* were inverted 'T' shaped and were often decorated with punched designs. An iron browband covered with *Pressblech* foil decoration was attached to the rim of the bowl. The lower rim of the browband was pierced at regular intervals to allow the attachment of a leather lining and the suspension of bronze cheek-plates. At the apex of the helmet was a bronze disc with a ridged knob protruding from the centre, from which a plume could be attached. The whole helmet was either gilded or silver-gilt.

Use

Since the head appears to have been one of the main targets of enemy blows (see Chapter 3), the possession of a helmet would have significantly increased a warrior's chance of survival. The helmet given to Beowulf by Hrothgar is described as having a wire-bound crest so that no sword could seriously injure him when he went into battle. The poet also describes how Wulf Wonreding survived a sword blow on his head that split his helmet, although he was knocked unconscious.

> *Ne meahte se snella sunu Wonredes*
> *ealdum ceorle ondslyht giofan*
> *ac he him on heafde helm ær gescer*
> *þæt he blode fah bugan sceolde*
> *feoll on foldan næs he fæge þa git,*
> *ac he hyne gewyrpte þeah ðe him wund hrine*

> Nor might the bold son of Wonred
> to the old man give an answering blow
> when he on the head first sheared through his helmet
> so that blood stained he was forced to bow
> fall to earth. Still he was not doomed to die yet
> but he recovered though the wound hurt him.
> (*Beowulf,* 2971)

However, no defence was proof against the most forceful blows; Beowulf's sword 'Hrunting' is said to have *helm oft gescær* 'often sheared through helmet' and Ongentheow is said to have killed Eofor *billes ecgum* 'with the edge of a sword' which *guðhelm toglad* 'split the war-helm'.

Furthermore, when attacked by surprise, warriors would have no time to don their helmets or mail but would have to rely on their shields:

þa wæs on healle   heardecg togen
sweord ofer setlum   sidrand manig
hafen handa fæst   helm ne gemunde,
byrnan side   þa hine se broga angeat

Then was in the hall hard-edged sword drawn
from above the seats, many broad shields
lifted firmly in the hand; none thought of helm
or broad mail-byrnie when he realised the danger.
(*Beowulf*, 1288)

5 The social context of warfare

Geongne æþeling sceolan   gode gesiðas
byldan to beaduwe   and to beahgife

The young prince shall   good companions
encourage to battle   and to ring-giving.
(*Gnomic Verse*)

It is impossible to fully understand warfare in isolation from its social context, as war is a social activity. However, the nature of Anglo-Saxon society, and consequently warfare evolved over time, from the many and confused 'kingdoms' of the early migrations in the fifth century, through the 'heptarchy' of the sixth and seventh centuries, to the establishment of a largely unified English nation in the late eighth and ninth centuries, firstly under the house of Mercia then Wessex. The trend to the centralisation of power reflected the regeneration of the urban centres and the gradual improvement in the road infrastructure.

The Warband

Swa sceal geong guma   gode gewyrcean,
fromum feohgiftum   on fæder bearme,
þæt hine on ylde   eft gewunigen
wilgesiþas,   þonne wig cume,
leode gelæsten.

So should a young man   do good deeds
give gifts of treasure   while under his father's protection,
so that when he is older   ever afterwards he will have
dear companions,   then when war comes
the warband will stand by him.
(*Beowulf*, 20)

Throughout this period the social and military structure was defined by the institution of the 'warband'. Every 'lord', whether king, *ætheling* or *ealdorman* would maintain a band of warriors and it was by virtue of the military prowess of this warband that he maintained his position.

The warband would comprise the lord's immediate kinsmen and the best warriors from the region. In addition a lord who was militarily successful, either in raiding his neighbours or forcing them to yield tribute, would attract warriors from outside the region, which would in turn increase his ability to raid and exact tribute. Bede records how the popularity of Oswine, king of Deira, was such that noble men came from every region to serve him. The social hierarchy of the warband appears to have been based on a combination of birth and ability. While good birth was a great advantage, it would appear that a successful warrior, even from a modest background, might be able to achieve high rank.

The warriors of the warband lived in the lord's hall. This cohabitation would be important in developing loyalty and an *esprit de corps* within the warband. In addition to eating at the lord's table, the warriors were rewarded for their service with gifts, particularly of weapons and armour, and, after long service, with grants of land. These warriors were in no way mercenaries however; the relationship between lord and his warband was long term and was considered to be honourable for both parties. Personal prestige was considered extremely important. The value of gifts given by the lord therefore lay not only in their monetary worth but also in the prestige they brought. Gift giving was both public and formal, and reflected well on both the lord, who demonstrated his ability to provide gifts, and the warrior who earned them.

In return for their lord's generosity the warriors accepted a number of social obligations. The most important of which was the duty to fight in the warband and, if their lord was killed, to avenge him or die in the attempt. The reciprocal nature of the gift giving and these obligations is summed up in the fragmentary account of the battle of Finnsburh:

> *Ne gefrægn ic næfre wurþlicor æt wera hilde*
> *sixtig sigebeorna sel gebæran*
> *ne nefre swanas hwitne medo sel forgyldan*
> *ðonne Hnæfe guldan his hægstealdas*

> Never have I heard of worthier that were at battle
> sixty 'war-bears' so bore themselves,
> never was bright mead so repaid
> than that Hnaef gave his noblemen
> (*Finnsburh*, 37)

If the lord was killed in battle the obligation was immediate, his warband must stand and fight until they were victorious or, as was more often the case, they were all slain.

> *þa wearð afeallen þæs folces ealdor,*
> *æþelredes eorl; ealle gesawon*
> *heorðgeneatas þæt hyra heorra læg.*

þa ðær wendon forð wlance þegenas,
unearge men efston georne;
hi woldon þa ealle oðer twega,
lif forlætan oððe leofne gewrecan.

Then fell the leader of the folk
Æthlered's earl; all could see
among the hearth-troop their lord lying dead.
Then went forth the proud thegns
brave men quick and eager;
all would have one of two things
to quit life or to avenge their lord.
(*Battle of Maldon*, 202)

Although the idea of dying in battle rather than quitting the field if the lord was slain was clearly an ideal that not every warrior would live up to, it should not be dismissed as fantasy. The *Anglo-Saxon Chronicle* records several incidences where warbands were annihilated with their lord, such as the battle of Daegsanstan in AD 603 where, despite the battle being an overwhelming Northumbrian victory, Theodbald, brother of Æthelferth King of Northumbria, was killed 'with all those he led of the army'. Analysis of recent military history has shown how defeat can lead to self-destructive or even suicidal impulses. This would be all the more likely following the loss of the dominant patriarchal figure within the tightly knit community of the warband, in which men had lived and fought together for many years.

At times the survivors were more pragmatic. In *Beowulf,* Hengest comes to terms with the Frisian king Finn following the death of his lord Hnæf at Finnsburh and Hrothgar is said to have come to terms with the Froda king of Heathobards to settle a long running feud in an agreement which included the marriage of Hrothgar's daughter, Freawaru, to Froda's son, Ingeld. In neither case was the peace sustained. In the spring following the fighting at Finnsburh, one of Hengest's men placed his sword *Hildeleoma* 'Battle-light' in his lap, a symbol of the obligation to seek revenge. Hengest broke the truce, killed Finn and all his men and took Hildeburh, Hnæf's sister and Finn's widow, back with him to Denmark. The marriage of Freawaru and Ingeld ended in no better circumstances, Ingeld was incited to revive the feud during a visit to his father in law and was cut down along with his warband by the Scyldings. Beowulf himself, as the archetypal warrior, made clear his opposition to such attempts at reconciliation and foretold their futility:

Oft seldan hwær
æfter leodhryre lytle hwile
bongar bugeð, þeah seo bryd duge.

> It seldom happens
> after the fall of a prince that for even a little while
> the spear rests, however worthy the bride.
> (*Beowulf,* 2029)

If the lord were murdered rather than killed in battle the obligation was to take revenge by killing either the perpetrator or the instigator of the crime. The obligation was enduring and such feuds could extend over generations.

The obligation to take revenge extended to other members of the warband. Beowulf rebuked the King Hrothgar '*Ne sorga, snotor guma; selre bið æghwæm þæt he his freond wrece, þonne he fela murne*', 'Do not be sorrowful, wise man! It is better for anyone that he should avenge his friend, rather than mourn greatly.'

The obligation to avenge a crime should not be viewed as anti-social. Rather it was a stabilising influence when no central authority existed to protect the individual. Without it each individual would have been vulnerable to acts of wanton violence, as there would have been no fear of punishment. However, the obligation frequently led to a *fæhð* 'feud' with a cycle of tit-for-tat killings. As a consequence, following the establishment of regional authority in the late sixth and early seventh century, a new system of *wergilds*, fixed payments in lieu of revenge, was introduced in an attempt to control this destructive cycle. It was not entirely successful in preventing feuding, however, so that King Edmund (AD 939-46) lamented the prevalence of feuds and laid down procedures for paying a weregild which were designed to prevent further outbreaks of violence by bereaved kinsmen.

The warband's loyalty to the lord appears to have transcended traditional kinship loyalties. The *Anglo-Saxon Chronicle* entry for AD 755 is extremely revealing. Cynewulf king of Wessex tried to expel a minor noble or *ætheling* called Cyneard. In response Cyneard and his warband of eighty-four warriors caught the king when he was visiting his mistress and killed him. The few warriors he had with him ran to help, despite being outnumbered. Cyneard offered to spare them but they declined and were all slain except one who was badly wounded. In the morning the remainder of the king's warband arrived and besieged Cyneard and his men. Cyneard asked them to accept him as king but they replied that they could never follow their lord's murderer. The besiegers then offered safe passage to any of his men, since many of them were related. They replied that they had made the same offer to the king's men, and were no more prepared to leave their lord than the king's men had been. The besiegers therefore stormed the enclosure and killed them. The difficulty of loyalties divided between lord and kin is a common theme in much of the surviving Germanic literature. The fragmentary passages of the poem 'Hildebrand and Hadubrand' describes how Hildebrand, a Goth and the champion of an army of Attila the Hun, was forced to fight his estranged son Hadubrand in a single combat because he would not come to terms.

Economic Structure

Æt .x. hidum to fostre .x. fata hunies, .ccc. hlafa, .xii. ambra Wilisc ealað, .xxx. hluttres, tu eald hriðeru oððe .x. weðeras, .x. gees, .xx. henna, .x. cesas, amber fulne buteran, .v. leaxas, .xx. pundwæga foðres 7 hundteontig æla.

From 10 hides as food, 10 vats of honey, 300 loaves, 12 ambers of Welsh ale, 30 of clear ale, 2 full-grown cows or 10 whethers, 10 geese, 20 hens, 10 cheeses, a full amber of butter, 5 salmon, 20 pounds of fodder and 100 eels.

(*Laws of Ine*)

To maintain a warband a lord needed a constant supply of commodities to support the warriors and gold and silver to give out as gifts. There were two ways in which these could be obtained. If the warband were strong enough they could raid neighbouring regions and either force them to yield tribute or just carry off valuables. Cattle were a particular target of this activity, because of the relative ease of driving them from one area to another. Since raids would often lead to battles, another type of booty would be the wargear of vanquished opponents (**68**). The pillaging of the dead is frequently mentioned in poetry; Ongentheow's body is stripped of his sword and helmet (*Beowulf*, 2986) and a Viking warrior attacks Byrhtnoth with the intention of taking his sword, armour and rings (*Battle of Maldon*, 160). It is not clear how these spoils of war would be divided, but it is likely that the majority would have been distributed among the participants in the raid with a proportion being retained by the lord.

Although raiding and exacting tribute feature highly in literature among the activities of the most successful kings, it cannot have been the major source of wealth as it is only a

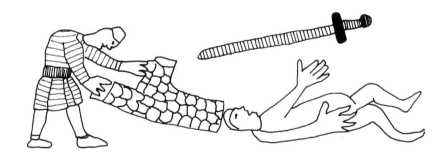

68   *One of several figures in the margin of the Bayeux Tapestry shown stripping the corpses of the slain of their equipment after the battle of Hastings. The wargear of vanquished opponents would have been an important source of funds with which a lord could reward the loyalty of his warriors.*
      (*Drawn by K. R. Dixon*)

method of redistribution not of production. The only creators of wealth were the agrarian population, who supported the king through the payment of 'food rents'. The king would travel around his kingdom on a circuit, with his warband, collecting some of the agricultural surplus from the population. The court would either stay with major landholders or on the king's own estates at royal 'vills'. How voluntarily these food rents were given up is open to question. It might be presumed to have depended on the degree of participation the population perceived themselves to have in their government. In regions where the population was tied to the king through kinship and where members of the population served in the warband the food rents might have been yielded quite voluntarily, especially as the king's visit would have been an opportunity to petition him. However, where the population had no personal ties to the king, the presence or threat of the warband would have been used to exact the levy. In recently conquered areas food rents would have been replaced by tribute, usually livestock on the hoof, which would be brought to the king. This was recognised to be a ignominious state, since the traffic was all one way, with no reciprocal access to the king. But in these regions a king would be unwise to visit except at the head of an army.

Land Tenure

þæs þe he me lond forgeaf,
mines fæder e þel, frea Myrginga.

After which he gave me land, my fathers estate, the lord of the Myrgings.
(*Widsið*, 95)

After long service higher ranking warriors would be given a grant of land to hold for the king. This is not to say that they would personally farm this land, rather, they would set up their own hall and gather their own warband and take food rents and service from their tenants. If the size of their landholding warranted it they might also have moved around on their own circuit.

In the early period such grants of land were generally made for the life of the recipient only and after his death reverted to the king, although the grant might sometimes be reaffirmed on his heirs. Such tenure was known as *lænland* or *folcland*. This gave the king a constantly renewable resource of land to give as a reward for service. Young men could only earn their land through service to the lord in the warband, not through inheritance.

The king would of course call on his nobles and their warbands to support him in battle. A military expedition or 'fyrd' would therefore be composed of several independent warbands. The king's own warband always remained a significant element of the army, however, for its warriors, by virtue of their personal ties, could be expected to engage the enemy aggressively. The same could not be guaranteed of the members of other warbands, since they would have only indirect loyalty to the king through their personal allegiance to their own leader.

This situation began to change in the eighth century due to the introduction of the concept of 'bookland' that was assigned with hereditary rights. Initially bookland was reserved for grants to the church for the foundation of religious institutions but gradually it also came to be granted to secular families and eventually hereditary tenure appears to have become the norm. Bede records how in Northumbria the introduction of bookland had a serious consequence for the social order. Whilst previously some land may have been held with hereditary rights, the widespread granting of land to the church by successive monarchs reduced the amount of royal land to such an extent that there was not enough to provide young warriors with endowments. Many such warriors were therefore seeking service elsewhere, where they would be properly rewarded, leaving the armies of the kingdom weak and unable to defend it.

At first bookland was granted free of all obligations to the king, but, as it became more prevalent this became untenable. In the mid to late eighth century the Mercian kings began to impose what were to become to be known as 'the three common burdens': bridge-building, fortification work and service on military expeditions in the 'fyrd'. The degree of service owed to the king depended on the size of the estate held, which was calculated in terms of 'hides'. In general each unit of five hides had to provide one man when the fyrd was called on, although local variations existed. However, it need not be assumed that the introduction of 'common burden' of fyrd service on bookland in some way indicates that there was a revolutionary change in the composition of the fyrd. The common burden merely re-established the right of kings to expect military service from landholders and quantified the numbers of men expected. The fyrd continued to be made up of the nobility and their personal retinues.

The Structure of Society

Æt twyhyndum were mon sceal sellan to monbote .xxx. scillinga, æt .vi. hyndum .lxxx. scillinga, æt .xii. hyndum .cxx. scillingum.

A two hundred man shall pay a manprice of 30 shillings, a six hundred (man) 80 shillings, a twelve hundred (man) 120 shillings.
(Laws of Ine)

The hierarchy of Anglo-Saxon society was defined in law. The fine for many crimes varied according to the rank of either the perpetrator or the victim. The most important of these were the fines paid for killing a man, the *wergild* 'man-price'. The earliest Kentish law codes recognise three main divisions, noble (*eorlcundne*) with a wergild of 300 Kentish shillings, free men (*frigne mann*) with a wergild of 100 shillings and three classes of unfree *læt* valued at 80, 60 and 40 shillings each. Slightly later West Saxon laws show a greater differentiation between the classes of free men, valuing the noble *geneat, gesið* or *þegn* at 1200 West Saxon shillings, six times that of the free *ceorls*, *gebures* or *gafolgeldan* 'taxpayers' with a wergild of 200 shillings, although a middle class, valued at 600 shillings, also appears occasionally. West Saxon shillings were certainly smaller than Kentish shillings but the exact exchange rate is unknown so it is not clear how these two scales relate. From this time, although the names used for each rank varied, this underlying structure appears to have remained constant for several centuries. Indeed, so common was the identification of each class with its wergild that the value was often used to describe the rank, thus *twelfhyndne mon*, 'twelve-hundred shilling man' and *twyhyndne mon*, 'two-hundred shilling man'. The wergild of the indigenous Welsh population was also recognised, but at half the value of the equivalent English rank.

The qualification for the status of a *þegn* 'thegn' is uncertain. A late law code states that a ceorl who owned five 'hides' of land acquired a thegn's wergild but that a ceorl who acquired a mail byrnie, a helmet and a sword but had no land remained a ceorl. However, thegn status also had a hereditary element that did not depend on ownership of land and it is clear that thegns could be landless.

The early law codes do not define the wergild of a king, an *ætheling* 'prince' or high ranking nobles such as the *ealdormen*, but we know from later sources they had a wergild several times that of a thegn. The late Northumbrian Law of Weregelds defines the wergild of an ealdorman as equivalent to that of four thegns and that of the king as that of fifteen thegns.

The unfree classes, generally known as *ðeow* or *esne*, had a status somewhere between servants and slaves, they were not free to move but they could own property and had a number of rights in law. Only free men, however, were entitled to bear arms. The law code of Ine, King of Wessex (AD 688-726), includes a list of fines for assisting the escape of another man's servant by lending him a weapon. Interestingly the fine is higher if the weapon is a spear rather than a sword, perhaps reflecting the common association in Germanic society of the spear with membership of the free 'warrior' class. The unfree came from three sources: a man captured in a battle or raid would be kept as a slave if he could not be ransomed by his kinsmen, a man might lose his freedom if he were unable to meet his legal obligations and the children of slaves would remain slaves.

There is considerable debate regarding the degree to which ceorls participated in military activity. The law code of Ine clearly ascribes military obligations on ceorls by defining the penalties if they did not meet them:

> *Gif gesiðcund mon landagende forsitte fierd, geselle .cxx. scillinga 7 ðolie his landes; unlandagende .lx. scillinga; cierlisc .xxx. scillinga to fierdwite.*

> If a *gesið* who holds land does not attend the fyrd he will give up 120 shillings and forfeit his land: (a *gesið*) without land (will give up) 60 shillings: a ceorl (will give up) 30 shillings as a fyrd-fine.

Victorian scholars saw these obligations as evidence of an egalitarian society, portraying the army as comprised of free husbandmen and representing the 'nation in arms'. More recently this interpretation has been challenged. It is contended that ceorls, if they participated in military activity at all, supported the army rather than serving in it. Evidence supporting this claim includes Bede's account of Imma, a Northumbrian thegn, who attempted to avoid capture following a battle by disguising himself as a *rusticus* who had been bringing provisions for the army. It is not clear, however, whether the Latin *rusticus* should be equated with a ceorl or with the lowlier ðeow or esne, or whether it was Imma's claim to be married and therefore clearly not a bachelor member of the warband that was important. The debate is further complicated by the fact that it is not possible to assess the proportion of society at each rank. Even if ceorls did form a significant element in Anglo-Saxon armies this need not indicate a 'nation in arms', if the greater proportion of the population were of the 'unfree' classes.

Manufacture of weapons

Beowulf maðelode   on him byrne scan,
searonet seowed   smiþes orþancum

Beowulf spoke his byrnie shone
a cunning net sewn with the smith's skill
(*Beowulf,* 405)

While simple items such as spearheads and knives were probably made by any smith (**69**), the manufacture of the majority of weapons, and in particular swords, was a specialist occupation. Despite their importance in Anglo-Saxon literature it appears from the law codes that the majority of smiths were not free men. The laws of Æthelbert of Kent allot a king's 'favourite smith' (*ambihtsmið*) the normal wergild of a free man, that is 100 Kentish shillings, but servants of the crown had higher wergilds than other men so it is likely that most smiths would have been ranked in the *læt* class. The client status of the smith is also illustrated in the laws of Ine which state that a nobleman who left his estate was allowed to take his smith with him, along with his reeve and his children's nurse.

Smith's tools are occasionally found (**70**). A unique collection of tools dating from the seventh century, probably from the grave of a smith, was discovered at Tattershall Thorpe, Lincolnshire. These included an anvil, hammers, tongs, a file, snips (shears) and punches.

The most famous smith in Germanic legend was Weland. The tale of Weland is known from later Viking sources, although he was clearly known to the Anglo-Saxons since he is mentioned several times in Anglo-Saxon poetry and depicted in a scene on the 'Franks' casket (**71**) and on a number of carved stone crosses. Weland is captured by the king Niðhad

69   *A detail from a tenth-century manuscript (MS Junius II) showing a smith working at his anvil.*

(Drawn by K. R. Dixon)

and is lamed by having the sinews in his knee-joints cut to prevent him from escaping. He is then set to work on an island to make precious objects for the king. Niðhad's two sons, motivated by greed, visit Weland in secret and he beheads them and uses their skulls to make drinking cups that he sends to the king. The king's daughter, Beadohild, has a ring that Weland had made. One day she breaks it and, afraid to tell her father, she takes it to Weland to have it mended. While he is working, Weland gives her beer to drink that has been drugged so that she falls asleep. While she is sleeping Weland rapes her, leaving her pregnant. He then escapes from the island using a flying-machine he has made; his revenge on Niðhad is complete.

There are numerous other references to Weland; Beowulf is said to own a marvellous mail byrnie made by him. In the poem *Waldere* the eponymous hero owns a sword named Mimming which he claims was forged by Weland and previously owned by both Widia, Weland's son (by Beadohild), and by Theodoric king of the Goths. Also. there are a number of places in England and on the continent associated with Weland, such as Wayland's Smithy, a prehistoric burial chamber in Berkshire.

Another famous smith in Germanic literature was Regin who forged the sword with which Sigurd slew the dragon Fafnir in the saga of the Volsungs. The saga tells how Regin forged two swords which Sigurd, because of his great strength, managed to break; only when he forged a third sword from the shards of the sword Gram that had been given to Sigurd's father King Sigmund by Odin and broken in the battle in which Sigmund was slain did Regin manage to forge a blade that was suitable for the hero. Sigurd tested the strength of the blade by striking the anvil on which it was forged and split it down to the stock. Then he tested its edge by throwing a lock of wool into a river and plunging the sword into the stream so that the wool was carried onto the blade and cut in two.

In the Viking period the blades of swords were sometimes stamped or inlayed with smith's marks. The two most famous smiths were Ulfberht and Ingelrii. Given the varied dates of blades bearing the marks of these smiths, they cannot all have been made by the two smiths personally; rather, it appears, either their names became 'trademarks' of the workshops in which they worked and continued to be used after their deaths or their names became synonymous with blades of good quality and were copied by smiths in other workshops.

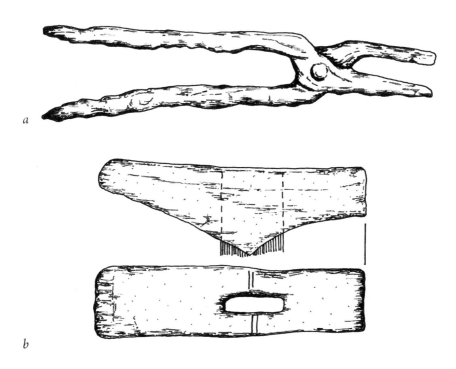

70   Smith's tools:
a   Tongs from Shakenoak, length 19cm.
b   Hammer from Thetford, length 13cm.

(Redrawn by K. R. Dixon after Wilson)

71   *A detail from the eighth-century 'Franks' casket illustrating the Weland Smith legend. Weland is shown working at his anvil making a cup from one of the heads of the king's sons. One of the headless corpses is hidden below the anvil. With his other hand Weland is giving a drugged drink to Beadohild, the king Niðhad's daughter.*

    (Redrawn by K. R. Dixon after Brears)

The values of weapons and other equipment were defined in both Frankish and Welsh law codes. The Welsh laws of the tenth-century king *Hywel Dda* listed the prices of a spear, a bow and twelve arrows and a broad axe all at four pence. A 'long' shield was twelve pence or twenty-four pence if it was decorated with gold or silver. The value of a basic sword was twelve pence and a 'white hilted' sword twenty four pence. The value of a sword with gold or silver on its hilt was not defined but was to be assessed individually according to the quality of the workmanship. These values should be compared to the prices of other goods listed in the law codes, for example livestock; a full grown ox was valued at sixty pence and a horse at one hundred and twenty pence.

The laws of the Ripurian Franks define the value of a sword and shield together at two *solidus* while a helmet is valued at six *solidus* and a mail byrnie at twelve *solidus*. These values can be compared to the normal wergild of a Frank of 200 *solidus*.

These values can also be compared to the time taken to manufacture modern reproductions. In an experimental forging of a pattern welded sword undertaken by J.W. Anstee of the Museum of English Rural Life, Reading, the time taken to manufacture the complete sword, including the scabbard and fittings was 74 hours.

6 The nature of warfare

Training

ða þær Byrhtnoð ongan beornas trymian,
rad and rædde, rincum tæhte
hu hi sceoldon standan and þone stede healdan,
and bæd þæt hyra randas rihte heoldon
fæste mid folman, and ne forhtedon na.

Then Byrhtnoth began to arrange his warriors
gave advice as he rode told the warriors
how they should stand and hold their place,
and bade that their shields they hold correctly
fast in their fists and not be afraid.
(*Battle of Maldon*, 17)

An important function of the warband would have been to train the young warriors. Evidence for formal weapons training is limited; the Danish chronicler Saxo describes how the hero Gram, when young, trained with experienced swordsmen, carefully copying their methods of parrying and thrusting. Saxo also describes how Swedish warriors continued to train in swordsmanship during a long period of peace until they were so skilled that they could graze an opponent's eyebrow with unerring aim. It should be noted, however, that Saxo, writing in the early thirteenth century, might well have been influenced by contemporary practices.

An important source of training appears to have been hunting and sports. Hunting in particular would not only have given the young warriors practice in the use of the spear and the bow but would also have accustomed them to killing. The hunting of potentially dangerous animals such as boars and bears, would also have accustomed them to a degree of personal risk taking, to working in a group and to relying on their comrades.

Sports such as wrestling, weight lifting and riding would have helped to develop the warriors' physical strength. This would have been very important as it requires significant strength to fight effectively with either a spear or sword and a shield for an extended period.

In particular, with a shield the unbalanced load and the position in which it is held require an unusual combination of muscles that are not developed in normal physical exercise.

One of the few references to the training of warriors in Anglo-Saxon literature occurs in the poem about the battle of Maldon in AD 991. We are told how Byrhtnoth the leader of the Saxon forces spent the last few minutes before the battle instructing his men how to stand in the shieldwall and how to hold their shields.

In the end, however, only through experience of battle could test whether a young man (*geoguð*) would in fact make a warrior (*duguð*). Hence the advice given in the poem *The Wanderer*:

> *Beorn sceal gebidan þonne he beot spriceð*
> *oþ þæt collenferð cunne gearwe*
> *hwider hreþra gehygd hweorfan wille*

> A man should wait before he makes a boast
> until his bold spirit knows through experience
> which way his heart will turn him.
> (*The Wanderer*, 70)

Scale of warfare

> *eofas we hatað oð vii men*
> *from vii hloð oð xxxv*
> *siððan bið here*

> Less than seven men shall be called thieves,
> from seven to thirty five are a band,
> more are an army.
> (*Laws of Ine*)

It should be recognised that 'warfare' varied in scale, involving individual combats and small skirmishes as well as sieges and full scale battles. Indeed, to an Anglo-Saxon there would probably have been little distinction between 'social violence' between neighbouring communities and war, except perhaps for the rank of the combatants. Even on its largest scale warfare in Anglo-Saxon England involved only relatively small forces. The law code of Ine which defines any force over thirty five men as an army is corroborated by abortive coup of the *ætheling* Cyneard in AD 755 which was conducted with only eighty four warriors. Descriptions of huge losses, such as 2065 Welsh dead at the battle of Beandun (AD 614), must, therefore, be considered to be an exaggeration.

Single Combat

Ane sweorde
merce gemærde   wið Myrgingum
bi Fifeldore   heoldon forð siþþan
Engle ond Swæfe,   swa hit Offa geslog.

With one sword
the border was set   with the Myrgings
by Fifeldor;   Henceforth it has held
between Angle and Swaefe   where Offa fought.
(*Widsið*, 41)

The smallest scale of 'war' was a single combat. This was an accepted method in Germanic society of settling a dispute between two individuals and single combat between two champions sometimes preceded a battle. The Danish chronicler Saxo described how 'the valiant commanders of old avoided executing their missions at everyone's risk where the issue could be settled by the fate of one or two'. It is unclear how widespread such duelling was in England but it is a common element in Viking sagas.

Single combats are also recorded among the continental Germanic tribes. The Roman historian Procopius records a single combat before the decisive battle between the Gothic army of Totila and the Byzantine army of Narses in AD 553. The result of the single combat does not appear to have obliged the army whose champion lost to come to terms, however. Rather the two opposing armies used the single combat as a test of their 'luck' before choosing whether to commit to battle.

The Vikings appear to have recognised two sorts of duel, *hólmganga* and *einvígi*. Hólmganga literally means 'island going' since duels were traditionally fought on islands. Saxo records a duel fought on an island in the River Eider by the fourth century Anglian king Offa which is also referred to in the Anglo-Saxon poem *Widsið*. An island would be an obvious setting for a duel since it would make escape or external interference difficult. Also, for single combat between the champions of two armies, a river might well mark the natural boundary of the tribes' lands. The Viking hólmganga was a formal affair fought with elaborate rules. The only account of the rules is given in Cormac's saga:

> It was the law of the hólmganga that the hide should be five ells long, with loops at its corners. Into these should be driven certain pins with heads to them, called tjosnur. He who made it ready should go to the pins in such a manner that he could see sky between his legs, holding the lobes of his ears and speaking the forewords used in the rite called 'The Sacrifice of the tjosnur.' Three squares should be marked round the hide, each one foot broad. At the outermost corners of the squares should be four poles, called hazels; when this

is done, it is a hazelled field. Each man should have three shields, and when they were cut up he must get upon the hide if he had given way from it before, and guard himself with his weapons alone thereafter. He who had been challenged should strike the first stroke. If one was wounded so that blood fell upon the hide, he should fight no longer. If either set one foot outside the hazel poles 'he went on his heel,' they said; but he 'ran' if both feet were outside. His own man was to hold the shield before each of the fighters. The one who was wounded should pay three marks of silver to be set free.

The idea of each duellist having a second who protected him with a shield was not universal and may be a misinterpretation of the rules regarding the exchange of shields that had been damaged. Nor was the prescription to fight only to 'first blood' always obeyed, many duels were fought to the death.

Because of the complexity of the formal hólmganga, the Vikings also recognised a simpler version or *einvígi*. In *Cormac's Saga*, Cormac challenges Bersi to a hólmganga. Bersi replies:

'Cormac, you have challenged me to the hólmganga; instead of that, I offer to fight you in simple sword-play (einvígi). You are a young man and little tried; the hólmganga needs craft and cunning, but sword-play, man to man, is an easy game.'

This is the type of duel fought without undue formality by Thorstein and Bjarni in the Saga of Thorstein *Stangarhoggr* (Staff-struck), after Thorstein killed three of Bjarni's servants in self defence:

Thorstein went outside and walked with Bjarni up to the hillock. They started fighting with determination and destroyed each other's shield. When they had been fighting for a long time, Bjarni said to Thorstein, 'I'm getting very thirsty now, I'm not so used to hard work as you are.'
'Go down to the stream then and drink,' said Thorstein.
Bjarni did so, and laid the sword down beside him. Thorstein picked it up, examined it and said 'You can't have been using this sword at Bodvarsdale.'
Bjarni said nothing, and they went back to the hillock. After they had been fighting for some time, it became obvious to Bjarni that Thorstein was a highly skilled fighter, and the outcome seemed less certain than he'd expected.
'Everything seems to go wrong for me today,' he said. 'now my shoe-thong is loose.'

'Tie it up then,' said Thorstein.

When Bjarni bent down to tie it, Thorstein went into the house and brought back two shields and a sword. He joined Bjarni on the hillock and said, 'Here's a sword and a shield my father sends you. The sword shouldn't get so easily blunted as the one you've been using. And I don't want to stand here any longer with no shield to protect me against your blows. I'd very much like to stop this game now, for I'm afraid your good luck will prove stronger than my bad luck. Every man wants to save his life, and I would too, if I could.'

'There's no point trying to talk yourself out of this,' said Bjarni. 'The fight must go on.'

'I wouldn't like to be the first to strike,' said Thorstein.

Then Bjarni struck at Thorstein, destroying his shield, and Thorstein hacked down Bjarni's shield in return.

'That was a blow,' said Bjarni.

Thorstein replied, 'Yours wasn't any lighter.'

Bjarni said, 'Your sword seems to be biting much better now than it was earlier.'

'I want to save myself from the foulest of luck if I possibly can,' said Thorstein. 'It scares me to have to fight you, so I want you yourself to settle this matter between us.'

It was Bjarni's turn to strike. Both men had lost their shields. Bjarni said, 'It would be a great mistake in one stroke both to throw away good fortune and do wrong. In my opinion I'd be fully paid for my three servants if you took their place and served me faithfully'.

It is not clear whether anything as elaborate as the rules for hólmganga were ever used in England.

Duels do not always appear to have been fought one against one. The duel fought by the Anglian king Offa was against two opponents, although this may have been exceptional as it was apparently to make up for a previous incident where the Swedish king Athisl was killed in a duel by two Anglian brothers, Keti and Vigi.

It appears that it was customary in a single combat to exchange blows alternately. This occurs not only in the formal hólmganga but also in the einvígi between Thorstein and Bjarni. Saxo mentions this custom:

> At the outset there was argument for a while as to which of them should make the first stroke, for in days of old when contests were arranged they did not try to exchange a rain of blows but hit at one another in a definite sequence with a gap between each turn. The strokes were infrequent but savage, with the result that it was their force, rather than their number that won acclaim. (Saxo II.56).

Saxo describes such a duel between Bjarki and Agner:

> Precedence was given to Agner because of his high rank, and the account has it that he gave a blow of such might that he clove the front of Biarki's helmet, tore the skin on his scalp and had to let go of the sword which was stuck in the eye-guards of the helmet. When Biarki's turn came to strike, he braced his foot against a log to get a better swing to his sword and drove the knife-edged blade straight through Agner's midriff. Some maintain that his dying mouth relaxed into a smile, a supreme disguise of his agony as he gave up the ghost. (Saxo II.56).

At other times duels appear to have been undertaken without any such formality. Saxo describes the duel between the Swedish king Athisl and Keti:

> … and giving as good as his word laid on with all his strength. Ketil met this with so stout a blow of his sword that it split the king's helmet and forced it's way to his head. Exasperated by this wound (blood was streaming copiously from his scalp) he went for Ketil with a volley of brisk strokes and beat him to his knees. (Saxo IV.97).

The belief that blows were exchanged alternately may have begun as a literary motif based on the natural rhythm of blow and counter-blow that occurs when fighting with a sword and shield.

Battles

> *þa wæs feohte neh,*
> *tir æt getohte. Wæs seo tid cumen*
> *þæt þær fæge men feallan sceoldon.*
>
> Then was the fight nigh,
> glory in battle. The time had come
> when fated men should fall.
> (*Battle of Maldon*, 103)

A battle was the decisive moment of a military expedition. Because of this battles are by far the most frequently recorded type of engagement in the historical records. It is likely that many more military expeditions did not culminate in any decisive action and were therefore not recorded. The decisive nature of battles meant they were a high risk option; the defeated force risked annihilation if they did not have a line of retreat to a defensive position. Battles, therefore, would only tend to occur when either the opposing forces were, or mistakenly believed themselves to be, of a similar size or, when a weaker force was caught by a fast moving enemy and forced to fight.

As an alternative to risking a battle a commander had a number of options. Depending on the cause of the conflict he might try and negotiate terms, such as the ceding of land or payment of tribute. Such settlements would often be accompanied by an exchange of hostages as an assurance of future good faith. Thus Oswy, king of Northumbria, attempted to buy off Penda, king of Mercia, prior to the battle of *Winwaed* in AD 655.

Another course of action would be to attempt to retire to a fortress or other defensible position. The enemy would then have three choices, assault the position, abandon the pursuit or lay siege. In the poem *Beowulf* the Swedish king Ongentheow is attacked by the army of the Geatish king Hygelac. Since he does not believe his own forces, who have just fought a battle against another Geatish army, can resist them in open battle he instead retreats to his fortress, which is on high ground and defended by earth ramparts. The defences are not strong enough, however, and the position is assaulted and Ongentheow killed.

Lastly, the army might simply disperse, making it difficult for the enemy to find them. Bede records how Oswin of Deira, realising the army of Oswy of Bernica was much stronger than his own decided not to risk an engagement at that time and so disbanded his army and sent all his men back to their homes.

Anglo-Saxons, unlike the Continental Germanic tribes such as the Franks and the Goths, do not appear to have regularly fought on horseback. The poem about the battle of Maldon in AD 991 makes it clear that many of the warriors had ridden to the battlefield but then dismounted and fought on foot. Indeed Byrhtnoth, the leader of the Saxons, gave orders to drive away the horses so that there would be no thought of retreat. Only his own horse was kept so that he could use it to ride around the battlefield. When Byrhtnoth was killed and a large part of the army routed one of the fugitives took his horse to speed his escape. Another account, albeit even later, is the *Anglo-Saxon Chronicle* entry for 1055. This records how the Herefordshire fyrd, in battle with the Welsh, fled before a single spear was thrown because they had been ordered to fight on horseback, contrary to their custom (*Anglos contra morem in equis pugnare jussit*). There are occasional references in Anglo-Saxon histories to mounted forces, such as the Northumbrian king Ecgfrith's expedition of horsemen (*equitatui*) sent against the Picts which is mentioned in the biography of Bishop Wilfrid. However, these do not make clear whether the force fought mounted or dismounted. *Equitates* is the general Latin term for mounted soldiers as opposed to the word *ala* which is used only of cavalry.

In battle both armies would mass together to form a 'shieldwall'. To be effective the shieldwall would have to be positioned so that it could not be outflanked. The smaller, weaker force would usually have some choice where to stand and fight and would therefore choose ground where natural terrain features, such as rivers, forests, bogs etc., made movement around the flanks of the line difficult or impossible. In this way they would

72   *Detail from the Bayeux Tapestry showing English warriors in a tightly packed
        'shieldwall' with shields overlapping. This formation may have been a response to
        being engaged by enemy archers. The number of arrows shown protruding from their
        shields indicates the intensity of the Norman archery. A diminutive English archer is
        shown skirmishing in front of the shieldwall and some of the warriors are throwing
        javelins and other missiles. The warriors in the rear ranks hold several javelins behind
        their shields. The tapestry consistently shows spears being used overarm both as missile
        weapons and in hand-to-hand combat. One of the warriors has a small rectangular
        banner or gonfanon on his spear, probably as a mark of authority.*

        (Drawn by K. R. Dixon)

be able to deploy in lines several ranks deep, largely negating the enemies numerical
superiority.

 A high proportion of Anglo-Saxon battles are recorded as taking place close to rivers.
Fords in rivers would be a natural place to intercept an enemy force moving into or
through an area and would also provide an excellent defensive position with both
flanks secure. Hence the many battles that are recorded as having taken place at fords:
Crecganford (AD 485), Cerdicesford (AD 519), Biedcanford (AD 571) and Beoford
(AD 752). Armies might also move along rivers, particularly if they had boats available
to transport their supplies. The river would then have provided at least one secure
flank and also a line of retreat if the enemy were not similarly equipped with boats. In
this way the Viking army of Anlaf escaped annihilation following their defeat at the

73   *Detail from the Bayeux Tapestry showing Saxon warriors defending a hill in a loose*
        'shieldwall'. The warriors have prepared their position against the Norman
        horsemen by emplacing spikes at the foot of the hill (not illustrated)
        causing the horses to fall and throw their riders.

        (Drawn by K. R. Dixon)

battle of Brunanburh in AD 937. A fork in a river could provide a strong position with both flanks secure. In AD 876 King Alfred of Wessex was forced to come to terms with a large Viking army that had taken up a strong defensive position between the River Frome and the River Tarrant in Dorset. Where high ground forced a loop in a river a natural fortress was created with only a narrow frontage with secure flanks and an advantageous position. Procopius records a Gothic army holding just such a position in a bend in the River Ister against a large army of Huns in AD 550.

If suitable terrain could not be found the weaker force would be forced to thin the line or risk being outflanked. If the shieldwall was too thin, however, it risked the enemy breaking through. The Bayeux tapestry shows men fighting in both a close formation (**72**) with shields overlapping and also in a much looser formation (**73**).

A battle would begin with archers and other lightly armed troops exchanging missiles. These scouts might begin by operating forward of their own shieldwall but would be forced back behind their own troops as the armies closed. Although missile weapons might be used to thin the enemy battle line and perhaps disrupt the

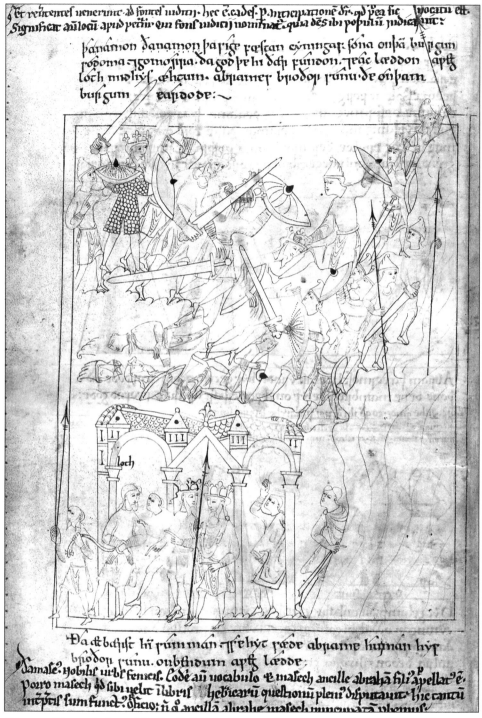

74   The confusion of the battlefield is illustrated in this scene from an eleventh-century manuscript (MS Cotton Claudius B IV f24v).
(Photograph courtesy of The British Library)

close packed formation, the defining moment of battle for the Anglo-Saxon warrior was when the shieldwalls met and blows were exchanged hand to hand.

The majority of the warriors would have probably been armed only with a spear and even the more wealthy warriors who owned a sword appear to have used spears initially. Gradually the opposing lines would be thinned as men were killed or wounded and fell out of the line. At this stage many of the injuries would have been relatively minor and wounded men would have often been able to escape to the rear. If one side felt itself to be at a disadvantage there might even be time to try to come to terms.

If the enemy line became disrupted the more aggressive warriors would attempt to make a breakthrough, using their swords to close on the enemy and cut them down. If the shieldwall was penetrated and could not be reformed then the remaining warriors would be forced to abandon the position or they would be cut down from behind.

Apart from the shieldwall the only other formation known to have been used, albeit infrequently, was the wedge. This formation (Latin *cuneus*) was used by the Romans and is mentioned by Vegetius in his *Epitoma Rei Militaris* written in either the fourth or fifth century:

> A wedge is the name for a mass of infantry who are attached to the line, which moves forward, narrower in front and broader behind, and breaks through the enemy lines, because a large number of men are discharging missiles into one position. (Vegetius III.19)

He goes on to say that the wedge is known as a 'pig's head' (*caput porcinum*) by the soldiers because of the resemblance to the head of a boar.

The use of the wedge in a battle between the Romans and the Sarmatians in AD 358 was described by the Roman soldier and historian Ammianus Marcellinus.

> The furious madness of this onset so angered our army that it could not brook it, and as the savages hotly menaced our emperor, ... they took the form of a wedge ... and scattered them with a hot charge. (Ammianus Marcellinus XVII.13.9)

The wedge is also mentioned in Viking literature and by the Danish historian Saxo. Saxo twice describes the formation, known to the Vikings as a *svínfylking* (**75**):

> ... in the first row he would put two men, four in the second, then increase the third to eight, and step up each succeeding rank by doubling the numbers of the one in the front. (Saxo I.32)

> ... he should divide his entire battle-line into three squadrons; each of these he should pack in twenties, but extend the middle section by

a further twenty men, arranging them to form the point of a cone or pyramid, and should bend back the wings to create a receding curve on each side. When a muster was held, he should construct the files of each squadron by starting with two men at the front and adding one only to each successive row; thus he would set three in the second line, four in the third, and so on, building up the following ranks with the same uniform symmetry until the outer edge came level with the wings. Each wing must contain ten ranks. Again, behind these he was to introduce young warriors equipped with javelins; to the rear of these he should place a company of older men to reinforce their comrades, if their strength waned, with their own brand of seasoned courage; a skilful strategist would see that slingers were attached at the sides, who could stand behind the lines of their fellows to assail the enemy with shots from a long distance. Beyond these he should admit indiscriminately men of any age or class without regard for status. The final battalion he ought to separate into three prongs, as with the vanguard, and deploy them in similar proportioned ranks. The rear, though connected to the foregoing columns, might offer defence by reversing itself to face in the opposite direction. (Saxo VII.248)

In both cases the secret of the wedge formation was supposed to have been given to the Viking commander by Odin.

As is made clear by Vegetius the wedge was intended to penetrate the opposing shieldwall so that the enemy could be attacked from the rear. Both Roman and Viking authors agree that the best way to defeat this stratagem was to form up a line in an arc or V shape, known to the Romans as a *forceps* or *forfex*, so as to envelop the wedge in a pincer movement (**76**).

Other tactics and formations may have been used although there is no direct evidence. The most likely tactic would be to attempt to encircle the enemy's flanks. The enemy's left flank was traditionally seen as the weaker, since the men attempting to outflank it could present their shields to the enemy. The terrain would also have a significant impact, however, and either flank might in fact be vulnerable. To counter such manoeuvres, and other stratagems, groups of men would probably be held in reserve behind the shieldwall, so that they could quickly deploy wherever they were needed.

Many of the most significant factors in the ability of the shieldwall to withstand the shock of battle would be moral rather than physical. The strength of the shieldwall depended on the willingness of the warriors to hold their ground while under attack and to put their lives in jeopardy by stepping forward into the front rank from the relative safety of the rear when other men fell. In war, with few exceptions, individuals are only able to withstand their natural instincts to run away because of the presence of their comrades, most importantly those they know well. They risk death only

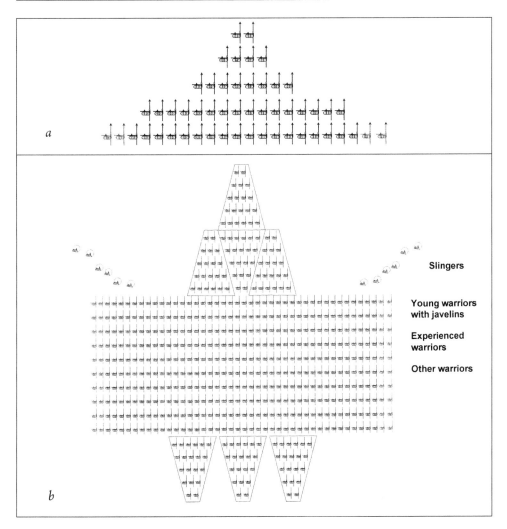

75   The Danish historian Saxo gives two different descriptions of the wedge or
      svínfylking *formation:*

a   *A broad wedge with each rank double the length of the one in front. The wedge
      projects forward from the shieldwall, here shown two ranks deep.*

b   *A more complex formation requiring very large forces. Saxo's description is difficult to
      interpret. The narrow wedge is formed of four squadrons, each of twenty men
      arranged with two men in the first rank with only one additional man added to each
      subsequent rank. The rest of the description may refer to the deployment of different
      troops within the shieldwall. Saxo says that this should be ten ranks deep with three
      squadrons of experienced warriors deployed behind. The importance of holding
      reserves of experienced troops to react to enemy outflanking manoeuvres and to
      strengthen the line if it became disrupted was stressed by the Roman strategist Vegetius.*

      (Drawn by R. Underwood)

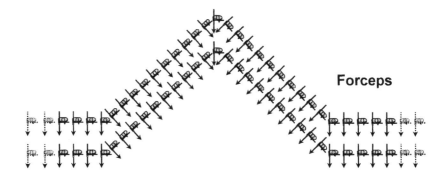

Forceps

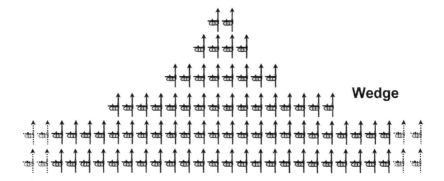

Wedge

76   Roman and Viking authors agree that the counter to the wedge or svínfylking
        formation was to deploy in an arc or 'V' formation so as to envelop the wedge. Roman
        authors refer to this as the 'pincer' (forceps or forfex) formation.

        (Drawn by R. Underwood)

because the alternative is worse, the complete loss of status within their small social
group from being branded a coward. The structure of the army, based on individual
warbands, would have been extremely effective in developing this *esprit de corps*.
Individuals would completely identify with their warband, having lived together in a
closed community for many years. In turn the army would be held together by similar
bonds between the leaders of the individual warbands and the king. If its leader fell in
the battle the rest of the warband would be obliged to avenge him or to die at his side.

During the fight each side would try to rouse themselves and intimidate their
enemies with gestures and shouts. The battle-cry of the Germanic tribes was known
as the *barritus* and was described by the fourth-century Roman historian Ammianus
Marcellinus:

This shout in the very heat of combat rises from a low murmur and gradually grows louder, like waves dashing against the cliffs. (Ammianus Marcellinus XVI.12.43)

Vegetius states that the battle-cry should not be raised until both lines have engaged each other as the enemy are more likely to be terrified if the shock of the battle-cry accompanies the attack; only inexperienced or cowardly men call out from a distance.

Ammianus also records how the Germanic warriors would 'sound the glories of their forefathers with wild shouts', a practice echoed six centuries later in the poem of the battle of Maldon where Ælfwine, son of Ælfric, recounted his lineage before promising to die rather than flee from the battlefield following the death of his lord.

If the shieldwall was broken or encircled groups of warriors might try to retreat to a place where they could reform. A battle between the Swedes and the Geats is described in the poem *Beowulf*. Following the death of their king, Hæthcyn, early in the battle the Geats were forced to retreat and were pursued by Swedes until they reached the forest of Ravenswood where they were besieged overnight. In the morning they were only saved by the arrival of a second Geatish army, otherwise they would have been attacked again and either cut down or hung if they surrendered.

If there was nowhere to retreat to, a rout would probably ensue as individuals and small groups scattered and attempted to outrun their pursuers. In a rout such as this the worst of the slaughter would have occurred, as is described at the battle of Brunanburh:

Wesseaxe forð ...
heowan herefleman   hindan þearle
mecum mylenscearpan.

The West Saxons ...
hewed the battle-fugitives from behind terribly
with mill-sharpened blades.
(*Anglo-Saxon Chronicle* entry for AD 937)

Skirmishes

If the number of combatants and the ground were such that an effective linear defence could not be made, any engagement would naturally develop into a skirmish. In addition skirmishes between opposing groups of scouts would be the natural precursor of any battle.

Skirmishes would differ significantly from battles between two shieldwalls. In a skirmish men would tend to fight individually or in small groups rather than as a formed body. The groups would usually form a loose 'skirmish line' with visual

77   *Two warriors engage in a single combat, a small part of a general melee. The lighter armed warrior with the axe closes on his more heavily armed opponent who has cast aside his spear and hastily draws his sword. A blow to the head such as this, delivered with force, could incapacitate or kill, even through an iron helmet. The warrior on the right wears a reconstruction of the ninth-century Viking helmet from Gjermundbu, Norway. He uses a hand-axe and carries a small (c.20in diameter) shield with a carinated shield-boss. His opponent wears a reconstruction of the late Roman helmet from Burgh Castle. He carries a large (c.36in diameter) shield. (Photograph: Author).*

contact maintained between each element. Each line would manoeuvre, attempting to gain a local superiority in numbers or position. If the enemy concentrated forces so as to threaten one part of the skirmish line it could give ground without losing integrity so that if the enemy advanced too far they would find their own flanks exposed to a counter-attack. Similarly, if the skirmish line was threatened by an outflanking manoeuvre it could simply be extended in response.

The preliminary skirmishes prior to a battle could be extremely important since, by preventing the enemy from observing their movements, the victorious army might well be able to lay an ambush. King Ecgferth of Northumbria was killed along with the greater part of his army having been lured into an ambush in a narrow mountain pass by the Picts in AD 685. This defeat was so total that Northumbria never really recovered and all the Pictish and Scottish lands that had been tributary were able to regain their independence.

It is likely that whenever possible local men would have been used as scouts since they would have had a considerable advantage because of their knowledge of the terrain. This is suggested by the obligation recorded in the post-conquest Book of Fees for the men of Cumberland to join the king's army in Scotland, serving in the vanguard when the army was advancing and the rearguard when it returned. A similar obligation is recorded in the Domesday Book for the town of Archenfield on the Welsh border.

This type of warfare must have placed a heavy burden on the personal courage of the men. They would have had to move and fight as individuals away from the moral support of their comrades and would have felt themselves constantly under threat due to the complex and rapidly changing nature of the battlefield. This morale aspect would have been as important, if not more so, than the actual sizes of the forces involved. A determined force that moved quickly and aggressively might be able to force their opponents to retreat even if they were numerically inferior.

78   *A ceorl attempts in vain to flee from a heavily armed warrior. The majority of casualties were usually suffered once the shieldwall was broken as the losing side triedto flee. The battle would dissolve into encounters between individuals or small groups of warriors; in such situations a ceorl armed with only a spear would be easily vanquished by an experienced gesið armed with a sword. (Photograph: Author)*

Sieges

*Her Ælle ond Cissa ymb sæton Andredes cester ond ofslogon alle þa þe þær inne eardedon ne
wearþ forþon Bret to lafe.*

Here Ælla and Cyssa besieged the fortress of Anderida and slew all those who dwelt
within, so that there was not on Briton remaining afterwards.
(*Anglo-Saxon Chronicle* entry for AD 491)

Even before the intensive phase of fort building in the eighth century, undertaken in response
to the threat of Viking raids, there would have been a number of fortified settlements in
England. The most formidable would have been based on Roman defences, such as the
Roman fort of Anderida at Pevensey, Hampshire, which was successfully besieged in AD
491 by Ælla and Cyssa (**79**). However, in general these defences were not maintained, so
that by the late seventh century the walls of Carlisle had decayed to such an extent that
they were regarded as a mere curiosity. An exception was York, where excavations have
shown that the Roman walls were repaired during the seventh century, although by AD
867 they had been allowed to decay again, so that when the Vikings were attacked there
by the Northumbrian armies of Osberht and Ælla the city was described as having neither
strong nor well-built walls.

Other settlements, particularly royal vills, would be protected by a wooden palisade.
The fortress of Bamburgh, a Northumbrian royal vill, is described in the *Anglo-Saxon
Chronicle* entry for AD 547 as having been first protected by a stockade, then by a
wall. Excavations at two Mercian royal vills at Hereford and Tamworth have revealed
the existence of ditch and palisade defences dating from the eighth or ninth century
on the same line as the tenth century ramparts. This is consistent with the imposition
of the 'common burden' of fortress work in Mercia in the mid to late eighth century
(see Chapter 5).

British kings also maintained fortified settlements defended by earthworks and
palisades. Many of these were based on hillforts that predated the Roman invasion.
Excavations have shown that a number of these hillforts were reoccupied in the late-
Roman and post-Roman periods. The largest of these is at South Cadbury, Somerset.
The extensive pre-Roman ramparts were refortified in the fifth century with a timber
fighting platform dressed with stone nearly 1200m (4000ft) long (**80**) and the
entrance defended with a gate-tower. The enclosure contained a number of buildings
including a royal hall 19m (62ft) long and 10m (33ft) wide. The fortress continues
in use until at least the late sixth century and must have been involved in the defence
of the area during the expansion of Wessex culminating in the battle of Dyrham in
AD 577.

There is no evidence that South Cadbury was ever attacked, however, the *Anglo-
Saxon Chronicle* records two battles that took place at nearby hillforts. In AD 522
Cynric king of Wessex fought against the British at *Searo byrg*, believed to be the

79 *The Roman walls of the fortress of Anderida (Pevensey, East Sussex) which was successfully besieged in AD 491 by the South Saxon kings Ælla and Cyssa.*

(Photograph: Author)

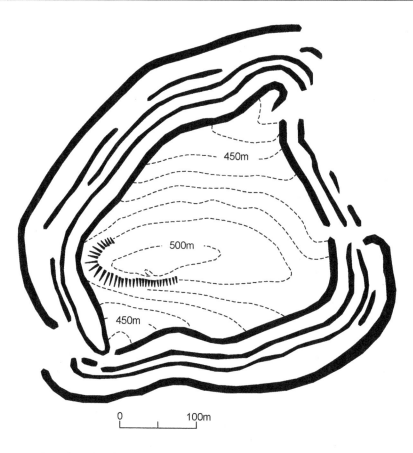

80   *A plan of the fortifications of the British hillfort at South Cadbury, Somerset. The pre Roman ramparts were refortified in the fifth century with a timber fighting platform dressed with stone nearly 1200m long.*

(Redrawn by R. Underwood after Alcock)

fortress of Old Sarum, Wiltshire. Four years later he again fought the British, this time at *Beran byrg*, Barbury Castle, Wiltshire.

Not all British fortified settlements were of this scale, however; the fortress of Mote of Mark, Strathclyde, is set on a craggy hillock and was defended by a timber reinforced stone wall. The area enclosed is only 75m (244ft) at its longest and 35m (114ft) at its widest. Interestingly, excavations showed evidence that the defences were destroyed by fire at some point in the fort's history.

Where a settlement was not fortified with a palisade the main hall could be defended, as occurred in AD 755 (see above). The defence of a hall is also a common literary theme. A fragmentary poetic account of a famous battle at the Frisian vill of Finnsburh describes in detail how the Danish king Hnaef and his warband of sixty warriors were besieged in a hall following the resurgence of an old feud. The warriors had been feasting and were awoken

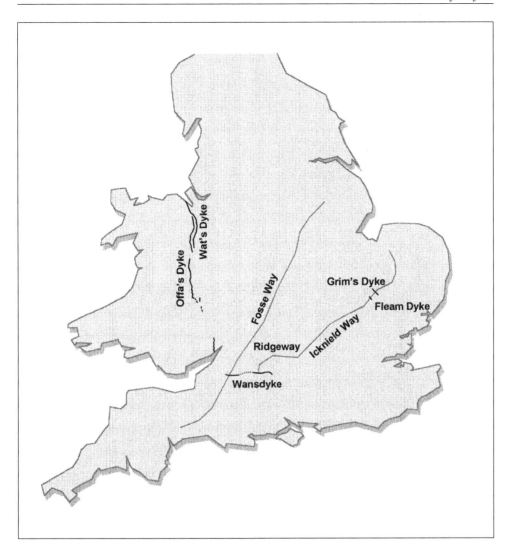

81   *Earthworks believed to date to the Anglo-Saxon period. Only Offa's Dyke, built to control the western border of Mercia, can be firmly dated. In the north it appears to have superseded a similar earthwork known as Wat's Dyke. Wansdyke runs from near Hungerford in Berkshire across Wiltshire and into Avon. The two surviving sections control North-South movement along the Fosse Way and the Ridgeway. Since the ditch lies on the northern side of the bank it was presumably built to protect against invasion from the north. Similarly Grim's Dyke and Fleam Dyke held a strategic position controlling access to East Anglia along the Icknield Way.*

by Hnaef who had heard the enemy approaching. They immediately ran to the two doors of the hall to stop the attackers getting in. The fighting was long and bloody:

> *Da wæs on healle wælslihta gehlyn*
> *sceolde cellod bord cenum on handa*
> *banhelm berstan buruhðelu dynede*

> There was in the hall the sound of slaughter
> curved shield boards held bravely in the hand
> bone helms (skulls?) burst the hall floor resounded
> (*Finnsburh*, 28)

The defenders held out for at least five days, until eventually a truce was arranged. In the fighting both Hnaef and the Frisian king Finn's son were killed.

An alternative to storming a fortress was to burn it down. Bede describes how in AD 651 Penda, king of Mercia, was unable to capture Bamburgh, either by storming it or by siege, and so attempted to set fire to it. He directed his troops to gather wood from the surrounding villages, pile it alongside the city walls and set fire to it. However, before the fire could take hold on the walls, the wind turned away from the city, driving the flames back on the men kindling it so that some of them were injured and the assault failed. Njal's Saga describes how Njal and his family were besieged in their hall following a long running blood-feud. When the besiegers found they were unable to overcome the defenders they were forced to burn the hall down.

A besieged force might still pose a significant threat and during a long siege the besiegers would be vulnerable to surprise attacks. Bede related how in AD 663 Osric, king of Deira, besieged the British king Cadwalla. The British force surprised their besiegers with a sudden sally, defeated them and killed Osric. For this reason, during extended sieges, besiegers may often have built their own defences, as the Vikings did when besieging Rochester in AD 885.

Some of the most enigmatic remains from the Anglo-Saxon period are the great linear earthworks such as Wansdyke in Wiltshire and Grim's Dyke and Fleam Dyke in Cambridgeshire (**81**). These cannot in general be accurately dated, except for the most well known, Offa's Dyke, which was built by the Mercian king Offa (AD 757-796). The defences ran for 240km (150 miles) along the English-Welsh border from the Dee estuary in the north to the river Wye in the south, using natural barriers wherever possible together with 130km (80 miles) of earthworks. In places the ramparts were 7m (24ft) high surmounted by a palisade together with a 2m (6ft) ditch (**82**). It is unlikely, however, that these defences were ever intended as linear fortifications. No Anglo-Saxon kingdom would be able to sustain sufficient forces to provide adequate defences for even a small part of their length. Rather they are likely to have served as 'trip-wires', ensuring that enemy raids were identified so that they could be intercepted by forces stationed in the interior of the kingdom.

82   *A section of Offa's Dyke near Knighton, Powys. The defences, built by the Mercian king Offa (AD 757-796), ran for 240 km (150 miles) along the English-Welsh border from the Dee estuary in the north to the river Wye in the south. Natural barriers were included wherever possible together with 130km (80 miles) of earthworks. These consisted of a 2m (6ft) ditch and ramparts which were up to 7m (24ft) high, surmounted by a palisade.*

7 Conclusions

Weapons

The weapons of the Anglo-Saxon warrior were part of a common heritage shared by all the Germanic peoples in northern Europe and Scandinavia. The parallel development of weapons in England and on the continent is indicative of the high degree of continuing contact. Much has been made of the 'Swedish connection' at Sutton Hoo, but it should be remembered that Sutton Hoo shows diverse continental connections including Merovingian coins and Byzantine silverwork. Indeed the trade routes stretched even further afield; cowry shells from the shores of the Red Sea and even ivory from Africa or India are regular finds in pagan Saxon graves.

This trade was not all one way; native styles developed in England and were exported to the continent. The English were as much involved in the artistic developments as their continental brethren. Perhaps the most striking example of an English export was the sword ring which originated in Kent in the mid sixth century. The early form of free running ring developed into a solid cast ring and by the seventh century could be found across Europe.

Despite the changes in the style of decoration, which often reflect more widespread changes in decorative forms used in metalwork, sculpture and illumination, there appears to have been little development in weapon technology from the migration of the Anglo-Saxons to the arrival of the Vikings. The basic weapons were enduring: spear and shield for the rank and file, sword, spear and shield for higher-ranking warriors. Only the very richest warriors wore a helmet or body armour.

If weapons did not change significantly, we might be forgiven for concluding that warfare did not change either. This would be to ignore the massive social developments that occurred as the diverse scattered communities of settlers coalesced into larger and larger kingdoms. For as these kingdoms grew so did the size of the armies they could command and the distances that these armies campaigned over.

In the fifth and sixth century, when kingdoms were made up of single tribal groups, an army would usually consist of a single warband, or perhaps two or three if the tribe had several 'kings'. The growth of the kingdoms increased the number of warbands that could be called upon. Men whose fathers had been kings in their own right became ealdormen or thegns and brought their retinue to fight for the king. At the battle of *Winwaed* in AD 655 the Mercian army of Penda which was defeated by the

Northumbrians was said to include thirty separate warbands each with their own leader.

The distances over which campaigns were fought also increased from the sixth to the seventh centuries. The sixth century saw the gradual westward spread of Anglo-Saxon control. The campaign of West Saxon kings Cuthwine and Ceawlin in AD 577 is one of the few sixth-century campaigns for which the places involved can be identified. Their victory at Dyrham led to the capture of three towns, the furthest of which, Gloucester, is 90 km (55 miles) as the crow flies from the West Saxon capital at Wilton, Hampshire. In contrast, in the seventh century, armies often campaigned over much larger distances; Northumbrian armies fought on the Welsh border at Chester, Cheshire in AD 616 and at Oswestry, Shropshire in AD 641, around 300 km (200 miles) from the Bernician royal seat at Bamburgh (**83**).

Warriors

The effectiveness of Anglo-Saxon armies is often denigrated on three counts, that they lacked cavalry and archers and that they were limited tactically to a single formation, the shieldwall.

Whilst it is true that the Anglo-Saxons do not appear to have used cavalry, this does not mean that they did not recognise and exploit the strategic mobility of mounted forces. There is no reason to believe that, from the earliest times, raiding was not done on horseback whenever mounts were available. Also, the importance of cavalry on the medieval battlefield should not be over emphasised. History is full of examples of infantry forces, well led, defeating a mounted enemy. Even the Normans, whose mounted knights won renown across Europe, recognised this; on many occasions the Norman knights rode to battle but fought on foot, just as the English did at Maldon and Hastings.

If the armies of the Anglo-Saxons were without archers this would certainly have been a significant shortcoming. On what basis, however, is this assessment made? There are numerous reference to archery in Anglo-Saxon literature: the Maldon poet mentions archery on three separate occasions. Archers also appear in art, for example on the Franks' casket and the Bayeux Tapestry. The main evidence against the widespread use of archery is the lack of finds of archery equipment from graves. Absence of evidence is not, however, evidence of absence. Even if bows were frequently deposited in graves, how many would survive? Arrowheads do occasionally survive, but many more may have decayed completely or only remain as a corroded mass, amorphous and unrecognisable.

As far as the tactics they used there is simply too little evidence to draw any conclusions. To understand how battles were fought would require evidence from narrative histories or military manuals such as those Byzantine authors have left us. Instead we have only a few enigmatic references in poetry:

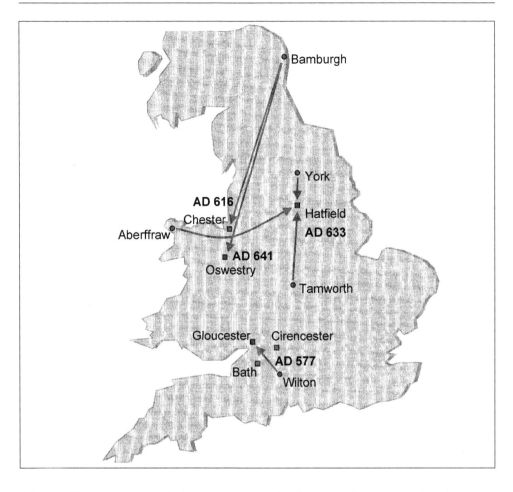

83   *The distances over which campaigns were fought increased from the sixth to the seventh centuries. The records of battles in the sixth century reflect the gradual westward spread of Anglo-Saxon control. The campaign of West Saxon kings Cuthwine and Ceawlin in AD 577 is one of the few sixth-century campaigns for which the places involved can be identified. The West Saxon victory at Dyrham led to the capture of Gloucester, Cirencester and Bath; Gloucester, the furthest of the three towns, is 90km (55 miles) as the crow flies from the West Saxon capital at Wilton, Hampshire. In contrast in the seventh century armies often campaigned over much larger distances; In AD 633 Edwin of Northumbria was killed at Hatfield Chase, Yorkshire in battle against combined forces of Penda of Mercia and the Welsh king Cadwallon. The battlefield lies only 40km (25 miles) from Edwin's capital of York but 115km (70 miles) from the Mercian capital at Tamworth and 235km (145 miles) from Cadwallon's principal seat at Aberffraw. Battles between the Northumbrians and the Welsh also took place on the border of Wales, at Chester in AD 616 and at Maserfeld (probably Oswestry, Shropshire) in AD 641, 280km (175 miles) and 320km (200 miles), respectively, from the Bernician royal seat at Bamburgh. (Redrawn by R. Underwood after Alcock)*

… he mid bordum het
wyrcan þone wihagan,   and þæt werod healdan
fæste wið feondum.

'He bade his men to make a war-hedge with their shields
and hold it fast against the foe.'
(*Battle of Maldon* 101)

For þan wearð her on felda   folc totwæmed,
scyldburh tobrocen.

'Then our force was divided on the field, the shieldwall was broken.'
(*Battle of Maldon* 241)

He bræc þone bordweall   and wið þa beornas feaht,

'He broke the shieldwall   and fought the warriors.'
(*Battle of Maldon* 277)

What lies hidden behind these words we cannot tell. For all we know they may have employed a rich variety of tactics within the basic concept of the 'shieldwall'. It is impossible to say.

In assessing the quality of the Anglo-Saxon army it is necessary to look beyond their weapons and tactics. Where the Anglo-Saxon army excelled was in the fighting spirit of the warriors. Throughout history this has always been recognised as the most important element in determining the effectiveness of a fighting force.

As is the case today, warfare was largely conducted by a military elite, who lived apart from the rest of society. The social structure, centred on the warband, was a critical element in the effectiveness of Anglo-Saxon armies. The close bond between the members of the warband, the *espirit de corps*, was essential if they were to face the horrors of battle. For, in the final analysis, men did not and do not fight for king or country but for the small group of men around them. They risked death because to run would have endangered their friends; the survival of the group had become more important than personal survival. Furthermore, to do otherwise would have meant disgrace and have led to exclusion from the group, perhaps even from society itself.

It can be argued that the whole of Anglo-Saxon society was focused on the development of this fighting spirit. Lords led and the warriors followed because of the personal ties between them. The poets taught the warrior ethos through the example of ancient heroes and promised to record the deeds of the group for future generations. All other members of society were peripheral.

The *espirit de corps* developed slowly, as the warriors spent their days together hunting and their nights together at the mead bench. The gifts the lord gave were not prized for their value alone but because of the prestige they carried. Status within the group was everything and was worth dying for. Time after time warriors 'earned their mead' defending their lord, standing by him in the shieldwall and, in the end, dying alongside him.

> *Hige sceal þe heardra   heorte þe cenre*
> *mod sceal þe mare   þe ure mægen lytlað.*
> *Her lið ure ealdor   eall forheawen*
> *god on greote.   A mæg gnornian*
> *se ðe nu fram þis wigplegan   wendan þenceð.*
> *Ic eom frod feores;   fram ic ne wille*
> *ac ic me be healfe   minum hlaforde*
> *be swa leofan men   licgan þence.*

> 'Thought shall be the harder   heart the keener
> mood shall be more   though our might diminishes.
> Here lies our lord,   hewn down,
> the good man lies in the dirt.   May he lament
> who now from this war-play   thinks to leave.
> I am an old man   I will not go,
> but beside   my lord,
> by that dear man,   do I think to lie.'
> (*Battle of Maldon*, 312)

Select Bibliography

History

Myres, J.N.L. 1986, *The English Settlements*. Oxford, Oxford University Press.

Stenton, F. 1971, *Anglo-Saxon England*. Oxford, Oxford University Press.

Weapons and Equipment

Bradbury J. 1985, *The Medieval Archer*. Woodbridge, The Boydell Press.

Swanton M. J. 1973, *The Spearheads of the Anglo-Saxon Settlements*. Leeds, The Royal Archaeological Institute.

Ellis Davidson H. R. 1962, *The Sword in Anglo-Saxon England*. Woodbridge, The Boydell Press.

Dickinson, T. and Härke, H. 1992, *Early Anglo-Saxon Shields*. London, Society of Antiquaries of London.

Tweddle, D. 1992, *The Anglian Helmet from York*. London, Council for British Archaeology.

Bruce-Mitford R. 1978, *The Sutton Hoo Ship Burial, Vol 2: Arms and Armour and Regalia*. London, British Museum Publications Ltd.

Warfare

Hawkes S. C. (ed.) 1989, *Weapons and Warfare in Anglo-Saxon England*. Oxford, The Oxford University Committee for Archaeology.

Pollington S. 1996, *The English Warrior from earliest time to 1066*. Hockwold-cum Wilton, Anglo-Saxon Books.

Alcock, L. 1987, *Economy, Society and Warfare Among the Britons and Saxons*. Cardiff, University of Wales Press.

Society

Evans, S. 1997, *Lords of Battle*. Woodbridge, The Boydell Press.

Abels, R.P. 1988, *Lordship and Military Obligation in Anglo-Saxon England*. London, British Museum Publications Ltd.

Hollister, C.W. 1962, *Anglo-Saxon Military Institutions on the Eve of the Norman Conquest*. Oxford, Oxford University Press.

Whitelock, D. 1952, *The Beginnings of English Society*. Harmondsworth, Penguin Books Ltd.

Literature

Swanton M. (trans.) 1978, *Beowulf*. Manchester, Manchester University Press.

Hamer R. (trans.) 1970, *A Choice of Anglo-Saxon Verse*. London, Faber and Faber.

Savage A. (trans.) 1982, *The Anglo-Saxon Chronicles*. London, Macmillan.

Sherley-Price (trans.) 1955, *Bede, A history of the English Church and People*. Harmondsworth, Penguin Books Ltd.

Ellis Davidson and Fisher (trans.) 1979, *Saxo Grammaticus, The History of the Danes*. Woodbridge, Boydell and Brewer Ltd.

Index